Faith Evolving

Faith Evolving

A Patchwork Journey

by

Trish McBride

Philip
Garside
Publishing Ltd.

First published in print 2005

By Patricia McBride, Wellington, Aotearoa New Zealand

Acknowledgements from the 2005 print edition

Grateful acknowledgement is made to the editors of the following publications for permission to reproduce articles, which first appeared in:
- *Tui Motu InterIslands* www.tuimotu.org.nz for Of Poppies and Vines, A Theology of Forgiveness, Trinity, Journey with the Jews, Millennium, The Emperor's New Clothes, A Quaker Saint, Community Care - the Good News, Ministering to Church Leavers, and Dancing with Gratitude
- *The Tablet* (London) www.thetablet.co.uk for The Invitation, Mother and Child, and Humility and Me
- *Vashti's Voices* for Living Springs, Discovering Decolonisation, The Violent Church, Reflections on a Transition, Transformation, and Another Response to Jacquie's Daughter.

The following were kind enough to give permission to use quotations:
- Preface: Carol P Christ, from *Diving Deep and Surfacing: Writers on Spiritual Quest* (1995)
- Sharing the Journey…: Sheldon Press, London, from *Soul Friend, A Study of Spirituality* by Kenneth Leech (1972)
- Appendix 1: Orbis Books, New York, from *Evangelization and Justice, New Insights for Christian Ministry* by John Walsh (1982).

Editor: Philippa Woodcock, Waikanae
Design: Stephanie Drew Design, Wellington

• • •

Republished 2024

International Print-on-demand paperback:
ISBN 9781991027719

Also Available
Print-on-demand paperback NZ & USA
ISBN 9798884062061

ePub / Kindle / Mobi eBook: ISBN 9781991027726
PDF eBook: 9781991027733

Philip Garside Publishing Ltd
PO Box 17160
Wellington 6147
New Zealand

sales@philipgarsidebooks.com — www.philipgarsidebooks.com

Contents

Acknowledgements

To my parents who gave me life and initiated me into the community of faith

To my children and their partners, of whom I'm very proud, and who have taught me much about love

To my grandchildren, in whose hands lies the future of our beautiful, hurting world

To my friends, who have loved and encouraged me, are beacons of goodness and integrity, and willingly share their strengths and needs

To the women, present and past, of ExAlt, Susanna Group, and the wider feminist networks, co-workers in promoting the well-being and spirituality of women

To other gatherers and shapers of fragments, for generous sharing of skills, ideas and materials birthright, convincement 'speak to your condition,'

To all the women of the world – until they live in peace and safety, there is work to be done

To all men who work respectfully for justice for all human beings

To those who have nurtured, taught, accompanied, counselled and challenged me on my journey of faith and healing

To staff at the Catholic Education Centre, Wellington, who gave me theological tools, awareness of the power of story, and later, help with research

To Philippa Woodcock, my editor, for gentle and meticulous choreography, and Stephanie Drew for the beautiful design work, the midwives of the whole project!

To Dr Ann Gilroy, Dr Anne Hadfield, Rosemary Neave, and Tony Pears for their encouragement

To Lighting the Fires Project Fund for the grant that enabled publication

Arohanui

Foreword

I do not remember these things
— they remember me.[1]

Janet Frame described a very personal experiential truth when she penned those words. After half a lifetime of extreme personal difficulty, her gift of writing finally emerged triumphant, and the writing itself served as a means of healing. Words have played an equally important role for Trish McBride.

Using the genres of poems, occasional pieces and articles, she has compiled an anthology which serves as a window into her personal spiritual and professional journey. With perceptive imagination she often uses metaphor to convey her meaning. We hear the joy of her discovery of goldfinches feasting on dandelions growing in the lawn, unmown in the chaos of disrupted routines ('Visitors'). The lack of adequate procedures and response, when client safety is compromised in institutions such as the church, is contrasted with the health protection measures that readily swing into place when a hepatitis outbreak is discovered in the community. Travelling in vineyard country in Europe, Trish suddenly sees a profound theological connection between grapevines twisted on their wires in a crucified shape and the words of Jesus 'I am the vine,' and she perceives how the little deaths of life can bear fruit ('Of Poppies and Vines …').

Intelligent analysis is evident in this collection, especially concerning the issue of sexual abuse in churches. 'Open Discipline, Consumer Rights and the Churches' is one example. Accompanied by theological reflections, such as 'Revisiting Original Sin,' these articles form a valuable resource for professional people in all churches. Trish herself has worked at the coal-face in bringing about more accountability for professional church workers at considerable personal cost. The subtlety of reactions to the fight for justice and liberation from oppression in this area is well described, for example, in 'Discovering Decolonisation.'

The material is divided into three sections, each prefaced with a reflection on how she perceives, retrospectively, her faith journey. The young adult Trish, who strived to fulfil the expectations of a traditional Catholic marriage and parish, has passed through the crucible of pain and loss by 2005 to become a mature and joyful Trish. The God, who at the beginning is a demanding figure evoking total blind surrender, is by the end the One who seeks justice in solidarity with marginalised women and men, and who manifests not only in creation, but also as the Quiet within.

Having journeyed a fraction of the way with Trish, I am delighted and awed by the transformation. While things may remember us, by God's grace and our hard work, they need not determine us, but become rich compost for our blooming.

Anne Hadfield PhD
Member, NZ Association of Christian Spiritual Directors
August 2005

Preface

The expression of women's spiritual quest is integrally related to the telling of women's stories. If women's stories are not told, the depth of women's souls will not be known.

Carol P Christ

The idea for this book arose from a chance comment by another spiritual director that there are few, if any, longitudinal studies of spiritual development. I realised that I could offer something of my own journey as a contribution to knowledge of this vital area of human existence. Piecing together this collection of 'patches,' written over a 30-year period, has been a fascinating task. Many pieces had been published in a variety of settings, then lay in sundry drawers and folders. Gathering up these moments of my God-journey has been another way of reminiscing, in a different realm from sorting the family photo album. The struggles, joys, sacred moments, ponderings, awakenings and eventual analysis and transformation all figure. It has been a journey into deep involvement with the church, and ultimately, a liberating departure. This is a journey many women have made in recent times, for their own unique reasons, and yet there are common threads.

The collection is not simply anthology, nor strictly autobiography, but reading between the lines will not be so difficult. The classic work of J W Fowler, *Stages of Faith: the Psychology of Human Development and the Quest for Meaning*, is relevant, with its analysis of developmental stages of faith (see Appendix 1). I can observe shifts in my perspective as fitting his descriptions, though in real life, stages and transitions are rarely clear-cut, and women's journeys do not necessarily follow Fowler's pattern. What is clear is the movement from my early adult years full of 'musts,' 'shoulds' and 'submission to the will of God,' through painful questionings produced by painful experiences, to a greater freedom and the reclaiming of my own inner knowing and voice. Not a simple transition, by any means! There have been tangles, mismatches and plain mistakes that have had to be unpicked and re-worked.

The written 'patches' have ultimately been my efforts to do theology. 'Faith seeking understanding' was a phrase I met much later. And each patch is a patchwork within itself, a gathering together of stories and knowings. In my days of caring for a large family I had christened my ponderings 'clothes-line theology,' the figuring out done as I pegged baby-napkins and a thousand socks out to dry. Questions such as: what does faith have to do with me as a woman? how, here and now, can I live this Christ-path? is love saying 'yes' or saying 'no'? what does forgiveness mean? how, in the context of the often chaotic family doings, were my beliefs relevant? Because almost all my formation and life have been in a Catholic context, those are the structures with which I have been most familiar, and most of the published material was therefore aimed at Catholic readership. Some items may raise questions for readers of other cultures, but I am confident that the essence of the journey is not unique to me or to Catholics! Countless others of all denominations have found their faith leads them into social action of some sort, and that churches can be unsafe places to be.

The years of needing to run to stay in the same spot are over. Amazingly, within all the hard work of raising a large family, and latterly as a solo parent, I was able to keep a record of the journey. And going with that part of the metaphor, perhaps an occasional cairn may be recognised by others, particularly by women whose paths have touched mine. Much of the early work was written so that I would not forget what I had noticed or felt. My God is a God who engages with me as I have wrestled with the hard questions of the realities of my own life and those of other women, a God who has been willing to be present to me in ways that have evolved with my maturing, a God who is firmly on the side of marginal people. This God is not confined to the Christian churches.

I had just finished my first literal patchwork quilt when I began to shape this book, and an in-progress section of my most recent one appears on its cover. The selecting and piecing together of the writings has in many ways paralleled that process. The light and dark, textured and plain fabrics in juxtaposition enhance each other and give the finished quilt its unique character. My hope is that other shapers of life-fabric, and in particular those who have left or may yet leave their churches will be able to relate to the issues, the challenges, and the changes that I have recorded in my life as a woman of Aotearoa New Zealand in the last quarter of the twentieth century and the beginning of the twenty-first.

Trish McBride

August 2005

Preface to the Third Edition

My purpose in assembling the first edition of *Faith Evolving* was two-fold: to fill a gap in the spirituality literature by offering a sample longitudinal study of an ordinary woman's journey of faith, and to encourage readers to reflect on their own journeys. This edition has the same aims!

A great deal has happened in the decade and a bit since 2005. Some things have changed, others remain constant. After seven years my time with the Quakers had run its course. Then followed seven years of with no faith community involvement, hermitting, I called it. But then after sporadic visits to St Andrew's on the Terrace, Wellington for other people's occasions over several years, I noticed a surge of joy each time I came away, generated, I realised, by the inclusive liturgical language, the Gospel-based social justice focus which I saw being lived out internally as well as externally, and the valuing of theological diversity. This Progressive Presbyterian parish works for me, and I'm happy to contribute there as fully as is congruent with my long-time refusal to sign up as member of a denomination. 'Post-denominational' suits me well! I am still awed and astonished, given my Catholic background, at being able to coordinate and lead an occasional Sunday service there.

My need to image and speak of the Divine as feminine was anchored and further validated by the Goddess pilgrimage to Crete with Carol Christ in 2006 and two subsequent trips to Divine Feminine conferences at a San Francisco Lutheran parish called herchurch. An extra delight there was dancing the Spiral with Starhawk and 1000 others. These tales are told in my book Exploring the Presence (2011). I believe women's need to image the Divine as feminine can be as soul-deep as men's need to image 'Him' as male.

There have been deeper connections with people of other faiths. In 2011 three friends and I facilitated a weekend on Compassion, where people from seven traditions brought a meditative practice from their understanding in which we could all participate. It was moving and enlightening. We discovered so much in common! And in 2014, as I stood awed with my tour group at the tomb of Rumi in Konya, Turkey, a Muslim woman took my hand, put a ring on my finger, embraced me and disappeared into the crowd. A startlingly beautiful experience of a Spirit-encounter! She had reached across the divide. The little green ring proves it did happen! These people, be they Shaman, Hindu, Buddhist, Daoist, Jew, Sufis, Neo-Pagan and that unknown woman have confirmed my hypothesis that all the various spiritual paths converge more closely as they more fully integrate the universal Divine Mystery. From one perspective, they are all culturally generated systems of symbols and metaphors pointing to the same Ultimate Reality.

Chaplaincy and counselling have necessarily been let go, and 'retired' now goes into that box on forms. Spiritual direction, giving and receiving, is still important. I write on when I have something to say. It has a been a privilege and pleasure to contribute to five Catholic-based theology books over the decade – on God images, wrong-doing today, prayer, social justice and eco-spirituality.[2] The process has been healing. I honour the

Catholic Church as my kohanga reo, my language nest. There I was well equipped for some steering of my journey and the reflection on it as it has unfolded.

The hard times are well and truly over and life is enjoyable and mostly peaceful. Good health helps with that, as do plentiful silence, solitude and simplicity – and more quilt-making. Another ten grandchildren have come along, all delicious buds on the family tree. It's fascinating to watch them unfold and see genes re-appearing over the five generations I've known. It is good to see how my adult offspring are able to help each other with their assorted skills. I am proud of them all. For me now Goddess/God permeates everything as Life-Force, and is personally communicating and relational in Jesus, my life companion, and is Holy Mystery. Perhaps this approaches what the Church Fathers were trying to get at when they defined the Trinity!

Trish McBride
September 2016

Clothes-line Theology
1974 – 1986

During the years 1974 – 1986, I was mostly concerned with home-making for a family that could mean ten to the table each evening, including our foster-daughter and the boarder. We had moved from the original home in Highbury, described in the first piece, to a much larger one, a couple of hills further north. Lots of work, lots of time for thinking during the relatively mindless tasks of matching hundreds of socks and in sit-down times for breast-feeding the latest baby. No time for reading!

A passion for 'that of God,' which had been with me since early childhood, found expression in a charismatic prayer-group which evolved into a covenant community – and so to immersion in the Scriptures. The discovery and enjoyment of this Book as Communication and potent source of metaphors and story templates led to its figuring largely in my writing of this time, especially as I tried to make sense of my marriage journey. And I had begun to think and write of my experience as a woman, and to protest at some of the traditional conservative concepts of women's role and duties. There was, though, a sense of the pregnancies, births and motherhood as sacred processes to be learned from and integrated into the spiritual journey.

Parish ministry was an outlet for my creative energy when there was a bit of time to spare. I was involved in Ministry of the Word, the Parish Pastoral Council, and later as catechist for the Rite of Christian Initiation of Adults through which people enter the Catholic Church. I really loved being a minister of the Eucharist both at church and during visits to housebound parishioners.

Later in this period, during weekend and eventually fully silent eight-day retreats, I began to discover a fascination with the interface, indeed at the heart of it, the common ground between religion and psychology. Reading Morton Kelsey's *Encounter with God* opened up a whole new world which made sense of and gave verbal shape to the Way I was experiencing God and the world. It was a time of visions and voices, and these experiences were reflected on and integrated into my understanding. They were quite normal in the charismatic culture as we lived it, though personally startling every time.

The Jungian-based Myers Briggs Personality Type Indicator was a revelation, a liberation. Until then I thought everyone knew what I knew and could do what I did, but there was so much more others could do that was impossible for me! Finding out that my preferred ways of operating were Introversion, Intuition, Feeling, and Judging gave me a toe-hold on solid ground that had hitherto eluded me, and I began to make sense of some of my recurring experiences. Finding out that there were gifts in this that not everyone had access to was an astonishment!

In retrospect, this time seems to have been, in J W Fowler's terms of faith development, mostly a late Stage 3 (synthetic-conventional), past the total dependence on external others for my connection with God, but still largely understanding and expressing this relationship in conventional terms. People at this stage are: 'acutely attuned to the expectations and judgements of significant others and as yet do not have a sure enough grasp of their own identity or faith in their own autonomous judgement to construct and maintain an independent perspective.'[2]

This period ended abruptly with the sudden death of my husband.

41 Koromiko Road

I came here for the first time as a visitor to afternoon tea one Sunday in 1960. Mount Pleasant Road seemed to be climbing to the sky, and as I looked out from one of the large picture windows we felt almost airborne over the city of Wellington. The McBride family had bought this house in 1959. Then, when we married in 1963, most of the others moved out and I moved in.

This piece is a memento of the house we lived in from 1963 to 1974. I am no less besotted now with the changing colours of Wellington than I was then!

In the distance about twenty miles away are the Orongo-rongos – or more officially the Rimutakas – fairly grim and bleak. They have a sprinkling of snow on them once or twice a winter – then we know it is really cold. One magic moment came after a very bad storm when in the late afternoon a pale sun came out and made the snow gleam with a weird orange light while the city and harbour were still lost in the murk.

We can see water and trees and nearer hills. From the French windows we can see the harbour and out towards the Hutt Valley, backed by the Tararuas. Kelburn hill blocks our view of Somes Island. Then out the front we see Oriental Bay, with Freyberg Pool jutting out into it, the boat harbour and the Overseas Terminal. To the south-east there is a minute part of Cook Strait framed by Pencarrow with its light-house and Karitane Hospital on the pine-clad hill of Melrose.

Before I came to Wellington from Tauranga, I was afraid there would be nothing green, but I was agreeably surprised. And here beside us, a source of joy and delight for the boys to play in, is a steep gully, the waterworks reserve. It has large glossy pine trees down the bottom, and up the sides a variety of native trees, pungas, ngaio, five-finger, and a liberal coating of blackberry spikes and honeysuckle, especially round the edges. It is inhabited by moreporks who converse on summer evenings, fantails who provide company up the path to Highbury Road, bright turquoise kingfishers, and for some years by a pair of lorikeets. These must have been escapees from some aviary, and are occasionally seen flashing past in a blaze of scarlet, green and blue. We thought we were seeing things the first time they appeared.

Te Aro Flat is spread below, and stretches out to Newtown to the south. Among the landmarks are St Helen's Hospital where all four children were born; Government House, the Governor General's residence, turreted and flag-poled among the trees beside the hospital; the museum with the Mount Victoria tunnel gaping over its left wing; the carillon whose notes float up on the calm beautiful Sunday afternoons which sometimes come as gifts after a spell of strong northerlies that slam doors, blow washing off the line, rattle windows and generally get on people's nerves.

The house can be approached from Highbury Road, which is an easier drive, but then there's a walk of 100 yards down the track beside the reserve. Anyone coming the other way, from Aro Street or Raroa Road can be seen from the front windows before they reach the stretch of Mount Pleasant Road immediately below us. They come into view again on Koromiko Road where it joins Old Bullock Road and Broomhill Road.

The section is long and narrow, on a steep slope. The letter-box is at the bottom and the house about one-third of the way up. Outside the back of the house on the left is a flat patch that should have been concreted but wasn't. It has a sandpit, a hose, a dustbin and a brand new fence erected after the wall blew down in a gale. On the right is a pocket-handkerchief sized lawn surrounded by an abelia hedge. It has the palest pink trumpet-shaped flowers in late summer and the bees love it. They land nectar-drunk on the porch in afternoon sun.

Up more steps to the clothes-line, and beyond that lies cowboy and Indian country, a few level spots, more bank, long grass, a couple of self-sown fruit trees, and the patch that an older neighbour had farmed for many years till he became too frail. Many's the basket of artichokes, beans, silverbeet, carrots we found on the porch by way of land-rent. In return, the boys took up all our old newspapers for their copper, invariably coming back with wide grins, lollies or a banana or orange. Also up the garden are various goat-tracks worn by our children and assorted neighbouring ones as they played, visited each other and grew up together over a nine-year period.

The house itself is not altogether conventional. Back and front doors open off the same porch. In the back door is a 'catador,' cut by mother-in-law for her pets, and later used by children not tall enough to reach the door handle when it was too windy to leave it open. A great Mummy-saving idea! It was named by our oldest to rhyme with 'matador.' Inside the front door is a black and grey lino tiled hall, the steps to downstairs, the glass door into the sitting room. This is long – 28 feet by 13 feet – has honey-coloured wood panelling at one end and French windows opening onto an unfenced sundeck at the other. There are the two large picture windows at the front of the house with the gas fire between them. The windowsills are low – just right for very small people.

The floor is polished (sometimes!) wood, which proved practical and easy to care for when the children were small. It would have taken a remarkable carpet to take all the traffic in this room. It is where the family lives. Television, radiogram, my spinning wheel and fleece, the chilly-bin (no cupboard or garage to put it in), the cocktail cabinet, lounge suite plus two extra chairs, two small tables, record cabinet, bookcase with my sewing on top, the pram, pushchair, a bed-chair, the big oak table and under it all the toys. There is a perpetual clutter round the edges of drawings to show Daddy, sticky block models, a pack of cards, photos, letters and anything somebody couldn't find another home for. And the cowbell, large, Swiss, sonorous, used for summoning children from round the neighbourhood at meal-times.

The kitchen where we eat is large. The walls are a creamy colour, with the top cupboards leaf-green and the bottom ones royal blue. There's a large electric oven in one corner and a stainless steel twin-sink bench next to it. The sun streams in on winter afternoons, and this is where I sew, with the baby, as the others did, sitting in her pram talking sometimes to me, sometimes to the washing flapping on the line.

The laundry has the same colour scheme – but a different lino, a relic of the time the hot water cylinder leaked down through the cupboard and along the floorboards lifting the green and yellow tiles before we'd realised anything was wrong. Then the back-door.

The bathroom opens off the hall between the front door and the lounge. The 'equipment' is all black – shiny black enamel. Quite a conversation-piece! The Dorchester Hotel in London also has one like that, so a chap told us who came to mend a window. So we were in good company. But I never liked it. Mainly, I think, because its walls were a bright daffodil yellow, and all the towels we got for wedding presents were pink. Once we'd painted the walls the palest possible pink and the other woodwork a darker shade, and put some muted green vinyl on the floor it was nicer to be in. With the toilet in the bathroom it did tend to get rather chaotic with seven people in the house. To have two will be much better!

The inside stairs are smooth grey painted concrete. A little odd, but wonderful for skittering down on an old blanket – a game discovered by our children when not very old.

Our foster-daughter's room is the first one at the bottom of the stairs – the sunniest and smallest bedroom. She came to live with us when she was ten, and baby number one was a year old. She has it to herself, but there is quite a lot of family stuff in it too. The games, a collection brought from Ireland in 1952 and now much used by the next generation, are in a drawer under her bed. There are Monopoly (Dublin version, and a Wellington version created by oldest son), Careers, Shipping, Aviation, Victory at Sea, Cluedo, Totopoly, Flutter and assorted jigsaws. It was the last room in the house to be re-decorated – she got most of the paper off one school holidays, but eighteen months passed before the rest got done. It looked so lovely when it was finished – a very pale greenish-grey paper with loops of white flowers. And a month later a blocked down-pipe on the sun-deck coincided with torrential rain and the window-frame leaked like a waterfall. Fortunately it dried without leaving much trace on the paper, but it did give us a few nasty moments.

The middle room had a series of long-term visitors, including a fellow Latin Honours student. Her boarding arrangements fell through just before finals and so she came to us. Her father, a nurseryman, gave us a generous and far-sighted gift of hedge plants to go right round the section. All three bigger children slept there later, the boys in bunks and their sister in a bed with the bedspread I crocheted for her. I'd economically used up all my wool scraps, but spent more on buying black wool for the edgings than a cheap bedspread would have cost. Still, it looked lovely when finished and was as warm as an extra blanket. With the three of them there, the room overflows with belongings: books and more books, two chests of drawers for clothes, the four 6' x 4' electric train boards, posters and certificates on the walls; a single wardrobe with three people's clothes, my sewing case, sleeping bags and the spare suitcase.

In the master bedroom, as I first saw it, was a green feature wall with a lattice of nasturtiums crawling all over it. Yuk! After many years, as with the bathroom, the horror disappeared. During a school holiday the children plus friends had a marvellous time stripping it off. They were allowed to draw on the denuded walls, and if the next paperers are thorough enough they'll find an array of drawings and messages comparable to the cave drawings of Lascaux. From the wall, Pope John XXIII beams benignly in memory of the papal blessing a priest friend requested for us on our wedding day. Because it gets no sun in winter for a couple of months I wanted a warm colour to succeed the nasturtiums. Pink seemed a logical choice. But after I'd got some sale-price paper for the hall – also pink – it was remarked that half the house seemed to be that colour! Baby's bassinet is beside our bed and when she is in her own room in the new big house we'll miss her sunny little face popping up in a morning from a night spent on her 'tum'!

We've had some very happy times here – our after-wedding party, my twenty-first birthday, and assorted parties – not so many, but enjoyable. Christmas Days with Grandma and Grandpa in a flurry of excited children and wrapping papers, and someone always a bit too excited for their own good.

We'll miss being able to watch the traffic in and out of the harbour, the rail-ferries like clockwork, the Rangatira (and the Māori and Wahine in their time), the opulent cruise ships, the occasional stark frigate or huge aircraft carrier, the orange container ships, oil tankers and Japanese squid boats, and the red nursemaid tugs, Kupe and Toia. And we'll miss the magic combinations of moon and water. Sometimes full, majestic and silver, orange or pink, with the reflection across Oriental Bay. Other times a delicate sliver with the morning star in tow in the no-coloured dawn over the black Tararuas.

And so to the new house, not very far away, where we can spread ourselves out, have enough cupboards for everything and watch the next part of our family story unfold.

Magnificat

Thank you, thank you, Lord.
Four weeks ago today our marriage was
fourteen years old.
We don't usually exchange tangible gifts –
It's too soon after Christmas.
But this year, Lord, you had other plans.
You surrounded us with your Love,
Enfolded enthralled us with your Love
And the word became flesh
And dwells in the inn of my body.
Thank you, Lord. Thank you, Lord.
At the beginning of the New Year I said to you
'Let me know your eternal plan for me for 1977'
So you have.
Thank you, Lord.
The other children are all precious
And I acknowledge your hand in their creation
We had a hand in it too
We waited, hoped and prayed.
But this time is different –
With a tender fatherly love
You have taken care of all the details.
Thank you, thank you, Lord.
You used the wild fluctuations of the tide of my body
To ensure we did not thwart your plan
You gave us this birthday present to celebrate our togetherness.
You even provided a car.
And then there's this incredible joy
That surpasses all logic –
But then, Lord, so do you.
May this consciousness
Of your creative, tender power and love,
Your here and now concern for us
Remain with us always
Through the months and years
And light the path our family is to follow
Thank you, Lord. Thank you Lord. Thank you Lord.

The new home was
blessed a couple
of years later with
a new pregnancy.
Baby number five,
and I was astounded
at the joy I felt.

Community

This daphne sprig gives you glory, Lord.
Your artistry is perfect.
I see two flowers open – the rest still buds,
Though the outer ones are beginning to unfurl.
The buds are closely bound together
On one stalk, in one calyx.
How can there be room for them all to open
To spread their four stiff waxy little petals
Without getting in each other's way,
Impinging on each other's freedom?
They are a community of your life in them
And even though I don't see how it can happen
By tomorrow the flowering will be full
To your glory!
And the fragrance of that community
Will give great joy.
Lord, teach me to trust you
To develop your life in the people I am closest to,
To trust that as a community
We are not going to get in each other's way
As we spread our petals,
To acknowledge that
All love, all beauty, all fragrance
Is a free gift from you
Thank you Lord!

I was on a weekend retreat where we were asked to choose a flower, and see what it said to us. Mine was positively eloquent! The poem later figured in a television documentary about retreat work.

Being Small

I looked deep into long-lashed eyes
That had seen three summers,
Saw echoes of myself
And promise of goodness.
I loved him
And yearned to give all I can give
To see that promise fulfilled.

Learning from
the small one.

I said to him 'I love you'
He looked deep into me,
Thought a moment
Checking out on all his experience
Then smiled and said
'Yes.'

So simply, Father, may I say 'yes' to you,
And thereby acknowledge
My security in your love.
Is this being born again,
Becoming as a little child
That I should discover my helplessness?

Babies are all 'yes'

To needs being met,
To caresses
To communication
To growth and learning.

On the other hand, a teenager
Becoming, in spurts, independent
Can hear with his ears a parent say
'I love you'
And toss straight back, honest in his confusion
'No, you don't!'

Father, let's have done with my adolescence
And my stiff-necked independent adulthood.
I want to become again a little child,
Your child!

A Blood Donor's Prayer

My thumb is sore, Lord,
Where the nurse jabbed it with the tiny blade
To check the haemoglobin level –
How did you feel after being thrashed with jagged hunks of metal?
And goaded up to Calvary by spear-points?
I wonder what your blood group was –
It must have been the same as your mother's.
They stripped you –
I rolled up a sleeve.
You were stretched on the rough wood –
I had a comfortable bed.
For you six-inch spikes and a hammer –
I had deft nurse, anaesthetic spray, sterile needle.
You were offered gall –
I was given coffee and iron tablets.
My offering a carefully measured 300 millilitres –
Yours – total, every drop.
My blood to aid one man, woman or child –
Yours, eternal salvation for every person ever born.
There is utterly no comparison.
And yet in the minutest way,
I have shared in your self-giving.
Thank you for the privilege.
Bless the nurses, technicians and doctors
Who deal with our blood, your gift of life to me.
Heal the person who receives it,
And as they are transfused with physical strength,
Transfuse them too with strength, peace and joy
Of your Risen Presence.
Amen. Alleluia!

A blood donating session in Easter Week generated this reflection.

About Loving

He says 'Love the others as I love you'
So how does he love me?
He is always available

always accessible
always accepting and encouraging
always forgiving.

If I kick and scream and throw tantrums, He waits
If I rebel, run away and harden my heart, He waits.
If I insist on my way not His, He waits.
Even if I forget my children, He will not forget me.
My name is engraved on the palm of His hand.
He loves me as much as the Father loves Him.
For me He gave up His throne in glory,
His human rights and dignity,
His health, strength and very life
To save me from myself.

He says 'Repent'

and 'Go and sin no more'
and 'Lay down your life'
and 'Take up your cross'
and 'Wash each other's feet'
and 'Where is your faith?'
and 'Didn't you know you can trust me?'

What a terrifying prospect!
I can't love like that – I'm human.

But then there is that most gracious act of love,
The enabling, or rather the Enabler.
When I put fear aside and start to live
Not I but Christ in me
I find that imperceptibly at first
Loving becomes possible,
Only because He gives me the power of His Spirit.
Lord, help me love as you have loved me.

'If you love
me, keep my
commandments,'
and 'Love' is the
commandment
that matters most.
How to actually
understand it?

If

If the power of the Spirit
Can transform inanimate flour-and-water wafer
Into Food, Sustainer, my Lord and God,
What miracle could be achieved
If I sign myself over
To be transformed and transfigured?
My hands to be His hands
My mouth to proclaim His peace, His Way,
My heart to love with His love,
My eyes to show His concern and reverence.
Lord, forgive me for all the times
Others have not experienced you in me,
And thank you for any times they have.

Then to look at it the other way,
How do I see you in others?
Sometimes it's so easy
To worship you present in a life
Given wholly, faithfully, triumphantly
To your service.
For that privilege in so many brothers and sisters
I thank you.
To see you present in lives in bondage
Is to see you bound and scourged –
Some comfort perhaps in my helpless presence.
To see you as a child in my children
Is to receive and serve you
Not just in daylight hours.

Always I must remember
That whatever I do to the least,
I do to you.
That means the least attractive,
The least responsive, the least grateful.
So I can't confine my loving to those
Who love me back and really appreciate me –
Even the pagans do that.

This sort of loving is only possible to you
And possible to me
Only if I give myself to you
Please take me, transform me,
So that I may know and serve you
In all I meet.

> What could I do for God while still up to the eyeballs in meals and laundry? Engage in the present reality!

Vine

You are the vine
And we are the branches.
You are saying –

> one form
> one purpose
> one life-blood

The branch must be recognisable as belonging

> must be true to form
> must fulfil the purpose, which is to bear fruit
> must allow the sap to flow from cell to cell to cell
> which is love received and given.

You are Love.

The Father is the husbandman.
He would know about grafting
Where shoots of vine are shaped and bound
together
To grow together into one
So that the strengths of each may flow into
the other
To enhance the fruit of both.
Is that how we are to be
With those who are closest to us?
Yet even in this life-sustaining closeness
We must not twine our tendrils into a
stranglehold
That hinders or chokes your life in others.

The branch has the right to call on the vine
For everything needed to fulfil its purpose.
As you commission us to bear lasting fruit
Anything we ask in your name will be given
As long as our purpose is your purpose.

And then you speak of pruning:
If we are to bear your intended fruit
We must offer ourselves in confidence
To the knife of Love –
Not a process to fear
If the end result is borne in mind.

Being 'vine' with
others can be a
challenge or worse!
How, in the context
of this image, to make
sense of difficult
relationships – and
in particular, my
marriage?

Only thus will Spirit-Life
Find fully responsive disciplined growth
ways.

You say you have pruned us by your Word
Was it as you slashed away
The rampant growth of human inclinations
In the Beatitudes?
Are we pruned in mid-winter death
So that the poor in spirit

> the gentle
> those who mourn
> those who hunger and thirst for
> justice
> the merciful
> the pure in heart
> the peace-makers
> the persecuted

Will be abundantly fruitful
In the joyous summer
Of your timing?
May we bear much fruit to the glory of
your Father!

Birth

When I was nine months grown
Things had to change.
For me to be released from the womb
Where I had been all-surrounded
All-nurtured, all-protected
Was trauma for us both.
Pain, strain, wound and emptiness –
Then joy at life not new, but in a new seen world.
Placenta, where our blood had pulsed together
In the closest touch two people can have
Served no purpose after birth.
I was freed of it.
Soon, in a year or thirty
My children, family and friends
Will give me another birth.
Now they surround me, love me, nurture me.
Then they must release me to a yet fuller, freer life
Where I shall see God.
They will have the pain, strain, wound and emptiness
But please, Lord, the joy as well.
Will it be for them a long wearing labour
Of a drawn-out illness
Whose end is an exhausted relief,
Or the suddenness of an elective caesarian
So much easier on the one being born
But maternal shock being deeper
And post-natal recovery taking rather longer?
You have it planned already, Lord.
You know best.
Placenta-body through which we've touched
Will have no further use then,
No function to perform
And so will be discarded.
I shall be living then more freely
Because for me you died and rose triumphant
And as my life goes on for ever
So will my loving.
Rejoice my friends, and be glad. Alleluia!
Release me and let me go. Alleluia!

At a large funeral
for a friend's mother
when I was seven
months pregnant, I
had suddenly sensed
the people gathered
there as a body giving
birth. And the image
continued to develop
as I thought of my own
death-birth.

Commitment

I am crucified to the world
And the world to me
It's no good saying
'I would be holier,
Or – pray more
Or – be more in tune with the Lord
If only …'

I am who I am
(He said that too)
And I am where I am –
With all that that entails
Of pain, restriction, turmoil,
And the nails of commitment
And being human
Holding me tight-fixed and bleeding
To the tossing tumbling wood of the world.

In this state He recognises me,
Loves me, sets my spirit
Resurrection free
If I am only still enough
To know that He is God.

Life was becoming more difficult, but the marriage vows were important. So I needed to engage with that reality too.

Forgiveness

How dare he make remarks like that?
They cut me to the quick.
And surely I'm entitled to my fury –
Adults just don't treat each other like that.
This was as bad as the time
She broke her word to me
Let me down when I trusted her
Or tried to, in view of all those other occasions.
It's pretty hard when you've learnt to expect it!
The hurt is real, undeserved
And grossly unfair
You see that, Lord, don't you?
I suppose I'm not perfect either,
But I am confident of your forgiveness.

What did you say?
It's conditional?
How come?
Oh, yes, there was that servant
Forgiven his own debt, then condemned
For refusing to forgive.
You teach us to ask for forgiveness
As we ourselves forgive.
Lord, I'm pretty slow –
If no-one ever hurt me
I'd have nothing to forgive
So in a way these hurts are privilege,
An opportunity to ready myself for forgiveness
And give thanks for that received.
They are indispensable to my learning process
And if I don't deserve the hurts –
How much less do you!
If by your power I learn to forgive
Even to the four hundred and ninetieth time
I am entering the mystery of your Cross.
Help me to forgive.

> What does forgiveness mean, particularly in the context of frequent hurts? Calling on the familiar Scriptures made sense at the time. Further work on this was needed in later years.

Al-Anon and a Catholic

The sole purpose of Al-Anon is to help the families or friends of alcoholics to live serene and positive lives in spite of the drinking problem of a member of the family. Alcoholism is a family disease which can twist the values, emotions and relationships of every member of an affected family. For many years I toyed with the idea of seeking help through Al-Anon, but held off for fear of labelling my spouse. Perhaps the alcoholic label wasn't really accurate? Perhaps the problem would go away? Perhaps I was over-reacting? Perhaps I was being disloyal? Perhaps …? But, eventually, largely because of emotional difficulties becoming evident in our children, I was forced to seek professional advice. And, again, eventually I found my way to Al-Anon. I wish I had taken the step years ago. All my fears proved groundless. There is a printed list of questions – not phrased 'Does your drinking spouse do this, that or the other?' but 'Do you …?' In other words, I qualified unmistakably by my own behaviour and reactions as a person who could be helped by and profit from the programme offered by Al-Anon.

This article was published anonymously after I spent time, rather late in the day, with Al-Anon, the 12-step programme for families and friends of alcoholics. It was my first experience of a spirituality that was not church-based. Writing this was my 12th step project.

Here is the full list of questions. 'Yes' answers to three or more would suggest that serious thought could be given to contacting Al-Anon.

1. Do you worry about how much someone else drinks?
2. Do you have money problems because of someone else's drinking?
3. Do you tell lies to cover up for someone else's drinking?
4. Do you feel that drinking is more important to your loved one than you are?
5. Do you think that the drinker's behaviour is caused by his or her companions?
6. Are meal times frequently delayed because of the drinker?
7. Do you make threats, such as 'If you don't stop drinking, I'll leave you'?
8. When you kiss the drinker hello, do you secretly try to smell his or her breath?
9. Are you afraid to upset someone for fear it will set off a drinking bout?
10. Have you been hurt or embarrassed by a drinker's behaviour?
11. Does it seem as if every holiday is spoiled because of drinking?
12. Have you considered calling the police because of drinking behaviour?
13. Do you find yourself searching for hidden liquor?
14. Do you feel that if the drinker loved you he or she would stop drinking to please you?

15. Have you refused social invitations out of fear or anxiety?

16. Do you sometimes feel guilty when you think of the lengths you have gone to control the drinker?

17. Do you think that if the drinker stopped drinking, your other problems would be solved?

18. Do you ever threaten to hurt yourself to scare the drinker into saying 'I'm sorry,' or 'I love you'?

19. Do you ever treat people (children, employees, parents, co-workers, etc) unjustly because you are angry at someone else for drinking too much?

20. Do you feel there is no-one who understands your problems?

I have come to realise that my own survival and serenity are indispensable to that of my children and will help my spouse. Dealing with myself is top priority. A parent travelling by air with children is directed in an emergency to put on their own oxygen mask before attempting to be responsible for those of their children.

The Al-Anon programme is based on the same twelve steps used by Alcoholics Anonymous, a book of daily readings, a number of slogans, and the Serenity Prayer. It is avowedly spiritual, but non-denominational, non-religious even, as the principles are adaptable to virtually any personal system of philosophy. However, I am a Catholic and as such I recognised with delight that a large proportion of the programme is the traditional teaching of the church – re-phrased, generalised, but the truth I know nonetheless. And I came to understand that for Catholics who live with a problem drinker a sound committed Catholic life seen through the lens of Al-Anon is a true recipe for sanity, wholeness – and even sanctity.

Let's look at the Twelve Steps:

1. **We admitted we were powerless over alcohol – that our lives had become unmanageable**
   That's the hard one – realising that the problem is beyond me. Tears, tantrums, even violence are to no avail, any more than trying to reason it away. I must learn to manage my own life and leave my drinking spouse to be responsible for his or her own.

2. **We came to believe that a Power greater than ourselves could restore us to sanity.**
   Basic to our belief is knowing a loving, powerful God, a caring Jesus, a consoling, healing, strengthening Spirit.

3. **We made a decision to turn our will and our lives over to the care of God as we understood Him.**
   By our Baptism and Confirmation we entered this commitment with God. And it has been the constant teaching of the church that a mature decision to thus surrender our wills and lives is a vital step in our pilgrimage to the Father.

4. **Made a searching and fearless moral inventory of ourselves.**
That is, examined our consciences in depth.

5. **Admitted to God, ourselves, and another human being the exact nature of our wrongs.**

6. **Were entirely ready to have God remove all these defects of character.**

7. **Humbly asked Him to remove our short-comings.**
These three steps are covered by our encounter with the healing Christ in the Sacrament of Reconciliation.

8. **Made a list of all persons we had harmed and became willing to make amends to them all.**

9. **Made direct amends to such people wherever possible, except when to do so would injure them or others.**
These are logical follow-ups to a sincere confession.

10. **Continued to take personal [moral] inventory and when we were wrong promptly admitted it.**
The effort to scrutinise our behaviour and attitudes is lifelong!

11. **Sought through prayer and meditation to improve our conscious contact with God as we understood Him, praying only for the knowledge of His will for us and the power to carry that out.**
This step is basic to life in Christ. Even ten minutes a day will give the Lord a chance to communicate what He has in store for us in the way of peace, love and strength. Half an hour is even better. And after a month or two of this routine I realised that it had become as necessary to me as breathing.

12. **Having had a spiritual awakening as the result of these steps, we tried to carry this message to others, and to practise these principles in all our affairs.**
Pass it on! Evangelise!

The book of daily readings gives wisdom drawn from many human and spiritual sources which throw light on different facets of how to live peacefully with oneself and an alcoholic. It is a real treasure and helps us in our exploration of the depth of meaning of the steps and slogans. Obviously, not everything is applicable to everyone, but most days the reading 'rings a bell' with me. Its truths have a much wider application, too. Any problem can become less devastating if I apply to it these same principles and slogans. Some of these are: *Let go and let God, Easy does it, Live and let live, One day at a time, How important is it?* Equivalents to most of these are quickly noticed in familiar Scriptures, for example: 'Be still and know that I am God.' To try to absorb these for use in a crisis is like doing a first-aid course. When trouble erupts, less energy has to be spent running up blind alleys or working out what might help. The rehearsed plan swings into action, albeit with the occasional hiccup! With an appropriate slogan to hold on to and the power of God to make the necessary actions possible, life can go on – yet again.

The Serenity Prayer is: 'God grant me the serenity to accept the things I cannot change, courage to change the things I can, and the wisdom to know the difference.' This is used to start and finish each weekly meeting. It, too, contains a wealth of significance. For me it was an eye-opener to realise that the wisdom to sort out the changeable from the unchangeable aspects in my life is something I do not automatically have. I must humbly ask for it. A prayer for wisdom is dear to God. If Solomon was so wonderfully rewarded for requesting wisdom, my prayer, too, will surely be heard.

Al-Anon, like the Body of Christ, has a human face. It is people, men and women of all ages and lifestyles. They have suffered a common experience and they want in terms of the Twelfth Step to pass on the help they themselves have received. They offer listening, unshockable acceptance, love and guidance. They, too, have wrestled with the problem of whether to trust the apparently untrustworthy, how to love the unlovely, how to explain the situation to the children with honesty and compassion. They are a real inspiration. I find it a privilege to be with people, particularly the teenagers, who are so honest, open and energetic in their efforts to get their lives into order with God as an integral part of each day. No-one ever considers that they have 'made it.' Even a decision for sobriety by a spouse does not automatically mean the end of adjustments. One set of difficulties will probably be replaced by another, and the programme will still be necessary.

Living unaided with an alcoholic is too much for most of us. Al-Anon offers the promise that living with peace, dignity and joy is possible. And God through the church promises us whatever grace we need to deal with our difficulties in His way. Gandhi, in the recent film, said: 'When you are tempted to despair, remember the way out is always the way of truth and love.' Christ is our way. And Al-Anon provides the shoes, staff and company.

Worth

Experts tell us our deepest need is to know
ourselves lovable
To know that we are of value
Not just for what we do but who we are.
In childhood and beyond we see ourselves
Largely as reflected in the mirrors of others' responses.
If the picture is distorted we tend to think
The reflection that of a distorted self,
Whereas it is as likely that the mirrors are misshapen
And damaged by their own inadequacies.
To laugh at myself as two-foot fairground
Dwarf or wave-shaped nine-foot giant
Is to assert my knowledge of myself as real
And reject the falsity of what I see.
To have Father God, not man, as point of reference
Is to accept a perfect image
Crystal clear and constant, of my value
He created me because I was His good idea.
He loves and cherishes me – I am precious in His sight
I am worth more than many sparrows
And not one of these falls without His knowing.
Jesus died for me, a sinner.
He considered me worth dying for!
Am I truly worth that much?
So this is where my value lies
The Father made me, Jesus redeemed me
And the Spirit will lead me into all truth.
The mirror of the world may show caricature,
But God sees, God knows, and God will judge
And still He loves me.

The inter-play
of faith and
psychology/
emotional health
began to interest me.
And God's love as a
source of self-esteem.

Cana

They came, the woman and her son, to celebrate
The marriage of two friends, the giving for life
of one to other.
Rejoicing, celebration and hospitality wavered in
consternation
As supplies of wine diminished and ran out.
Some mis-calculation of the steward's?
Or a mix-up in the guest list?
Or did some just drink more than their share?
Whatever the reason, the distress of hosts at impending disaster
Was noted by the woman, who whispered urgently
'Son, they have no wine.'
A brush-off, so it seemed: 'My time is not yet come'
But undeterred she primed the servants to obey without question
The command that would come as grape follows flower-fall.
Rich wine of love came forth from earthen jars,
With sparkle, colour, taste, bouquet beyond imagining –
Because she asked.
He might have done it anyway, or any other way.
So for his coming too:
God could have come as full-grown man
Or foundling child upon a throne.
But he chose to become a son, her son.
And chose at marriage feast to begin his wonders
Because she asked.

He chose for us through her to work the miracle
Of bringing back a marriage from the dead
Gave us a Mother shared to make the peace.
From the water of grim determination and readiness to forgive
He has poured out for us
The wine of love, of joy.
It bubbles and leaps from living springs within
As we rejoice in the Spirit of Love –
Because she asked
Alleluia!

Woman

In the fullness of His time
God offered to entrust His Word to Woman
That she might bear Him within
And give Him to the waiting world.
As the Eternal Heart received her 'Yes'
The Eternal Yes was spoken within her
And took flesh.
This once accomplished, Joseph's task began:
To protect and nurture under the Lord's direction
His Work, His Word in Woman.
Not to delegate or dominate or even mediate,
But to cherish in awe, the Spoken Word,
God's act.
Not to father the child, but to foster the child,
To tend the garden of the sapling Word
Till by the world this Word was heard.
May our men see truly as curse on Eve,
Not creed, their need to lord it over us.
We are all redeemed, but by each other freed
Must enter into our inheritance.
Mary is intercessor, prophet, priest
Her son, the Lord, refuses not her asking.
In her silence we meet that Word of Love.
Herself and precious Son were given without reserve
On the altar of Calvary
She was the first of a new generation of Temples
Wherein there dwelt the presence of the Almighty.
Yet this Temple to Herod's Temple came
To offer Son and doves.
No appropriation of authority there,
Only this: My soul glorifies the Lord,
My spirit rejoices in God my Saviour.
He looks on His servant in her lowliness
Henceforth all ages will call me blessed.
The Almighty has done great things for me.
Blessed are you among us, Mary.
May Father God plant in our hearts too
The Seed of His Word
And may your Son be the fruit of our lives.
Amen.

The prayer-group/ community where I learned so much was beginning to move towards a literal fundamentalist understanding of 'male headship,' as per St Paul's dictum 'the husband is head of the wife.' I could not go there!

Fruitfulness

By baptism I am pregnant with the Redeemer
Father God gives growth
to this Person within me –
But I must nurture this life
And feed it from my own supply of strength
And offer my stillness that I be filled with Peace.
I must diminish and He increase.

There are times in this gestation
When I rebel at what it's going to cost –
The nausea, exhaustion, heart-burn
And the sheer inconvenience of carrying Another
Whose knees and elbows prod my tender places.
Yet unless I commit the ultimate blasphemy
Of uprooting Him
and casting Him from my life –
Which is after all my own –
There are the times of unimagined joy;
At first the knowing but not yet feeling,
Then the first butterfly touches of perceptible feeling,
Hearing for the first time the heart-beat,
Reality of this other Life,
Others' awareness of a radiance from within,
Acknowledgement of another will
That sleeps when I'm awake, and wakes when I want sleep.

For me to be redeemed I must give birth to this Redeemer
And that hurts.
It is necessary, purposeful, the joy is there –
But it hurts.
He must break forth so that others
May cradle Him in their lives
And know the power and joy of newborn Love.

I had not yet met the 13th century mystic, Meister Eckhardt, or his question: 'Of what use is Christmas if he be not born in me?' But my experiences of pregnancies and births continued to converse with my Christ-journey.

Honoured

I am precious in His sight
I am honoured and He loves me!

He honours me

> through the fantail flitting round my tree
> through the kitten purring on my lap
> through sun-warmth through winter window
> through foetus fern fronds uncurling between rocks
> through diamond drops on perfect spider web
> through the perfume of a rose
> through gale-whipped trees releasing yellow leaves
> through pink buds bursting to sycamore green.

He honours me

> through the smiles of friends
> through the tears of friends
> through service given by others in His name
> through hugs and kisses from my children
> through the caring of my spouse
> through the privilege of watching people grow
> through His hurting Body that needs my love.

Yet should all these pass away, and sense,
The greatest honour of all would be there still:
He has given Himself to me as Kinsman-Redeemer
As Way, as Light, as Truth
As Bread of Life, as Living Water
As Goal, as Companion
As Strength, as Power
As Man, as God
As Love.
Thank you, Lord.

A gathering
up of precious
moments,
snapshots and
God-images!

Retreats

There was and is
A God
In Himself completely perfect, perfectly complete
Then because He is Love
And Love must find expression
He wanted to give each of us a sharing
in His own Life
So the flawless God created in Himself
An incompleteness, a space;
And in His infinite graciousness
Having created us, invites us to be part of Him
To take part in Him
To partake of Him
To complete the circle of Love
By accepting the invitation.

His desire for us is not that we sit
In the safety net of the Law,
But with the life-line of prayer around our waists
Set our feet on the ladder of living His Word
Heeding not the fearful cries
'You'll fall – it's much too dangerous!'
Then on His call to leap
In trust towards the outstretched Hands
To play, exult and thrill with Him
On the high trapeze of Love.

How does it all work? What does the God-Love-Life map look like? Again, retreats provided the space for deep reflection.

Incarnation

I lived for forty years and more
Inside this lumpish clayey body
Regarding it, largely with distaste,
as 'it' not 'me.'
Then in various ways there dawned on me
New recognition of the dignity of flesh,
my flesh.
In prayer Jesus came to me as humble
loving servant
And as I lay paralysed and helpless on a bed
Would wash me head to toe with love
Panic melted to assent – I had to trust His love.
Then piece by piece I was bathed in love
by Love
The goodness and beauty of Father God's design admired
And shown to me as planned for me from the beginning
And knit together in my mother's womb
Though taught still thunderstruck and awed
How I felt for Simon Peter. Perhaps he felt for me!

What did it mean to be embodied? Particularly in the light of this rather shocking prayer experience! Peter had got off lightly – and he'd had problems with having just his feet washed! Seeing my body through the eyes of Jesus was definitely not my idea. But how healing!

The humanity of sense, sensation, bone and nerve, muscle and blood
God's gift of creation to each one of us.
Designed to be at one with soul in worship like David as he danced
Condemned to pain and death by Adam's sin
When Jesus came to earth became redeemed
As embryo flesh, foetus flesh, boy-child flesh and man
The infinite perfect Word added to himself our earthly limits
As if that were not enough to dignify forever
The nature of mortal flesh
He gave from bread his God-man flesh to be our food
Food that gives eternal life, the immanent life of God
And his Spirit too, till then enthroned in Temple
Of marble, cedar beams, precious stones and beaten gold.
He sends in his new time to live within this flesh
Wherever a yearning soul creates a home.
Why should this flesh of mine be honoured thus as dwelling for my Lord?
And the Body of Christ, his church, is incomplete
Without my flesh-lived love for other Temples.
Though decay of death awaits, my body will at the end of time
Be raised and glorified and in perfection not known here
Know God.
For so many marvels, I thank you, Lord
A wonder I am, and all your works are wonders.
Thank you for my body.

Fishing

I came and said
'Here I am, Lord, have your way, Lord.'
Though in my pride I thought
I haven't had time for too much sinning.
He said 'Cast out your net again
Into the sea of your soul.'
And stunned I watched as we hauled in
A bulging net of sin –
Some slimy from the sea-bed sludge,
And others really quite appealing,
Shiny, sleek and silver.
'I am sinful, Lord. Depart from me.'
But he didn't go.
And so we named the names
Of the flapping, gasping, gaping throng,
And in the sunshine of his love they threshed no more.
Let's go, he said, 'Leave all this here.
Come walk with me and I will be
Your river of life, your living spring
Your Lord!'

Another retreat gave rise to this and the following three reflections. Being away for a fully-silent eight days was a wonderful opportunity for a rest, for sustained prayer – and for meals cooked by someone else!

Duckling

Quack, Lord.
You were there when I opened my eyes.
You tenderly broke open my shell.
You are the first one I saw –
You are my Mother.
I have no choice but to waddle after you
Quack, quack
Alleluia!

It was spring and the duck family on the stream gave me an image.

Hunger

Remove the distractions of everyday life, then one discovers what is really going on.

The edgy pain inside me felt like loneliness
And as so often in the past, I pushed it down
Back down into its box, then sat upon the lid
Pretending it would disappear if long enough ignored.
But newly knowing my need to feel and be
I risked unleashing all the imprisoned pain
And with decision up flew tight-bound lid
Then came a violent billowing forth
Like parachute blown by Spirit-gale
Through everywhere within, of hunger
Hunger for love.
No chance now to restrain, to gather up and stow away
Pain of emptiness, ache of need, bottomless pit
Hunger for Love!

'Come to me' says Love who wants to feed and fill me.
But how to know the breadth
And length and height and depth
Of all His love
If first I have not plumbed the depths
Of this great yawning chasm of emptiness
Essential pain and precious void!
Fill me, feed me, Lord.

He made each of us thus hungry
Hoping we would know in Him the source of food and love.
But no, we elsewhere seek our satisfaction
Mistaking ache inside as need for things and power
When all the time the yearning Christ
Says to our starving world
'Here is my Body, here is my Blood
For you to eat and drink.
I long to feed you with Myself
So that you'll know the fullness of my love.'

Please fill me, feed me, Lord
Fill me, feed me
I'm so hungry, Lord
And now I know my hunger is for You.

Encounter

Each day the soul-friend gave to me the Word
For breakfast, lunch and tea,
And in confidence, knowing the Power,
Launched me oar-less onto the river of Love
And was there each tomorrow
To hear where we had been.
My widow's mite of time and love and offering
Was received by our amazing Lord,
And he poured on me from his rich store
Not just blessings but himself
As awestruck, honoured, cherished and loved
I journeyed through time, myself and space
And knew him there.

A symphony of love he played for me:
Refrains and themes that started with a Word,
Or came as from a far-heard reed
Or pulsing drum mistaken for my heart,
Then taken up, developed in the prayer,
My own and that of church as gathered there.
With melodies that interwove the music grew
In power and harmony and emergent rhythm,
Through gentle love and learning pain
To cymbal-clashed crescendo of exultant joy.

He freed me from my chrysalis
So moth-like I must seek the Light
Whether through darkness of desert and death
Or through new fields of new-sprung flowers
Only this: to seek him and be found by him
 to love him and be overwhelmed by Love.
Betroth me to yourself, Lord. Maranatha!

The themes and converging images felt as though I was in an already choreographed production, and all I needed to do was respond.

Burdens

I'm weary, Lord
With all the weight of other people's burdens.
Sometimes it's satisfying seeing new growth
and freedom
But often it just goes on and on and on
Then I want out.
Maybe you too felt like that
As you staggered and fell
Under the weight of my cross and burdens
It was too much for your strength
Already drained by scourge and crown.
But you got up and kept going
Because that cross was in the end to be for me
A sign of glory and redemption
You knew full well what you were offering
In the time before:
'Come to me all who labour and are heavy burdened
And I will give you rest.'

Sometimes, back at home, it all seemed too much like hard work, especially when people needed much long-term support through difficulties. And my own had reappeared.

And now your promise is for me.
That Calvary road must be my way to Easter joy
As you received my load with willing love
So must I for others
And when I fall exhausted
The Simon-strength to rise
Will be from you.

After That

1987– 1994

Being widowed in 1986 simplified life in some ways and left it open to further complications in others. My primary role during these next years was being solo parent of a still-large family with all that entailed. I learned two important lessons: to ask for support as I needed it (receiving is a whole heap harder than giving!), and that the best gifts I could give to others were time and love. Being on a widow's benefit was not conducive to much concrete gift-giving.

My horizons widened beyond home and the parish as I became a part-time industrial chaplain in various corporate settings. I learned much through relating to a wider variety of people and situations. Two of the main strands of this time were some formal study of the theology and practice of ministry, and a dark, silenced journey that took me to the brink of suicide. The time of visions and voices faded and God was 'silent' and 'absent' for long periods.

In 1994, working as a co-facilitator of a learning group with women who had been subjected to domestic violence provided me with a whole new vocabulary, the concept of structural analysis, and an introduction to Paulo Freire. His teaching on education as a tool of liberation and the concept of critical thinking fitted well with my own questionings, as did *The Kairos Document: Challenge to the Church*, which came from South African theologians in 1985.

As this period developed, so did the necessity for having a look at the givens, at the church and at its male God. Ministry and my own journey threw up hard questions, and the answers I'd grown up with no longer worked: Why do we/they think that? How did it get like that? What got me into these situations? What were the scripts or Scriptures that kept me there? From whom does the truly healing support come? And the primary answer to the last question for me was 'from women outside the churches.' They were the ones with the responses that made sense.

This period saw the shift to Fowler's Stage 4: Individuative – Reflective Faith: 'In addition to the kind of reflection on one's previous … system of values … there must be … a relocation of authority [on religious belief] within the self.' The individual critiques previous beliefs and structures.

Eventually my perception grew of a too-wide gap between church proclamation and its praxis on some of the tough questions it faces. I had done my years of feminist working for change. I was regularly going home from mass on Sundays with a headache from all the 'buts,' the male God-language, and trying to translate the creed into something I could say with integrity. The headache was the physical manifestation of the sense of banging my head on a brick wall. After a final and fundamental disagreement with the hierarchy I left. The concept of the church as a safe and healing place where one discovers the voice and invitation of God had crumbled. God as God's-self continued to be central to the journey. With relief I discovered sister-Lancastrian Edwina Gateley's words:

> 'God ran away
> when we imprisoned her
> and put her in a box
> named Church.'

'God ran away' in
I Hear a Seed Growing

Change

How can I write a poem
About the ugliness of relief
At the amputation of a gangrenous leg?
(Health will come, the throb recede
And I will walk again.)
Or about the pain

— of the last conversation that embodied the rejection of all the years

— of the sympathetic widows murmuring gently 'I know how you feel, dear' (like hell they did, but no point now in shattering their illusions of 'such a lovely family')

— of discovering debts and getting the bill for being lied to and cheated

— of desperate efforts to recapture a picture or memory of the good times

— of seeing the pain in a friend's eyes as she told of the peace and joy and love she'd had with her man who'd just died too

— of not missing him

— of all the letters that spoke of a cheerful, capable, generous man, and the fear of going mad because my reality was too different (how I loved the two with honesty who wrote 'you must be confused')

— of children's scarred lives – please heal them, Lord

— of my helplessness to penetrate his fear and anger and make him feel loved

— of choosing a single grave and not wanting to visit it ever again

— of getting rid of clothes too fast

— of waking up in a nightmare sweat after seeing him come back

— of trying to reconcile a healed, forgiven soul with my ongoing pain and anger

— of feeling relief not deprivation at bed-time

— of taking off my rings – it's over now!

— of learning to walk tall

Now that the time of leaning into the teeth
Of an icy wind is past.

Father, forgive him, he didn't know what he was doing to me.
Father forgive me, I still don't know what I did to him.

'The grieving process is more difficult where there has been a complex love-hate relationship.' This statement, made at a bereavement volunteers' course, was an anchor during a most difficult time. My church family and many others gave huge support. To very few was I able to acknowledge the sadness of the realities.

Garden

He whispered to me 'My garden!'
And that, being no gardener myself, was mystery
Until I let the seed of his Word sink in
and start to grow.

Then I began to see how he'd come
To a patch of clayey mud
And chosen it to be transformed;
Had staked his claim, fenced in secure,
Then dug and channelled and drained the soil
Made fertile with his sweat and flesh and blood,
And having planned his garden-scape,
Breathed his Word into the secret places
Of my life.
Then waited and watched.

He smiled to see new shoots
And growth and buds;
Bloodied his fingers uprooting briars of sin
Framed the vines and staked the flowers
That could not stand the force of winds;
Lit warmth of friends as oil pots
To see me through the frosty nights;
Pruned and pruned and pruned some more,
Repaired the ravages of storms,
Burnt dead wood, watered me from springs of living love.
All this with tender care, persistence
And full knowledge of the seasons
Of my life.

If he now joys to be in me
Finds pleasure in some fruit and fragrance there
So be it.
The Gardener is my delight
Thank you, Lord.

An invitation in a book of prayer exercises: call Jesus your special names for him – then listen for his special name for you. Initial reaction to my new name: huh?

Ruach

The clouds that sail and scud along
Do not resist the ruach wind
That shapes, carries, blows;
Not rooted like the trees
Nor yet rootless
But free in the element of their being
To be changed and move and fly,
And then to fall as rain-Word
To water the earth and make it yield
Thus feeding the hungry.
Then having achieved what they were sent to do
To return, be changed, be blown
Be free again.
Lord, draw me up into your love.
Let me be lamb-gentle white,
Sun-gold, blood-red, or purple-grey with promise
As you will.
Teach me to fly.

Just loved meeting the Hebrew word 'ruach' that means wind / spirit / breath / life. And freedom beckoned – including my embryo career as an industrial chaplain.

Gold

I sat to pray with a chrysanthemum
Huge and shaggy gold –
No longer a child with the daisy
'He loves me, he loves me not'
And the tension of how it will turn out –
But as woman, with confidence,
As each petal, every one,
Said 'He loves me'
And when lap and floor were strewn
With love-words
Still the flower was undiminished.

Another flower prayer, not daphne this time but a chrysanthemum.

Integration

'Look and see within yourself the Lazarus
The buried one, the lifeless one
Whose rotting stench
Needs holding in with heavy stone;
The self that was ignored, or sick too long,
Or put to death and buried.
Let Jesus call her forth.'

So now He's here.
I've wept with Him about the death within
Trust Him to love dead sister-self to life
To glorify the Father's name.
He calls on me to roll away the stone
And let his power in.

'Come forth!' He says
And sensing power at work
I watch and feel the stirring of the dead
Blind groping and reeling towards the light
'Unbind her, take all ties away
And set her free.'

So in obedience gentlest hands
Release the bonds and wash away the smell of death,
And feed me food of love,
And hold me close till balance comes
And the weakness of the tomb becomes new life.
Alleluia!

At the beginning of a bereavement counselling relationship with a minister from another denomination I felt huge hope for a good future. My understanding grew that the spiritual and the emotional/psychological are not separate, and that the stories of Scripture provide powerful templates or metaphors for our real lives.

Storm

I am
I am Lord
I am Lord of the storm
The storm within

When water-spouts of memory gush from the depths
To swamp the boat of conscious life
And waves of emotion charge and choke your breath
I am the Lord

When visibility is nil, the charts and compass lost
The sandbanks moved, the beacons gone
And sense of direction disappears
I am the Way the Truth
When your sail of self-control's in shreds
And horizontal rain and gale
Needle tears from heart and eyes
I am the Lord

When ingrained patterns of behaving fly
apart
Shattered by the water force, filling your
boat
And fear of drowning saps all will
I am the Life

When arms are lead and blistered hands
Have no more fight against the tide
Then rest in me
I am the Lord

For at my Word the storm will still
The glory of the ever-present sun break
through
The beauty of the promised shore appear
New strength and wholeness will be yours
Let me be Lord

But the
counselling went
wrong, badly
wrong.

And continued
to do so

Chaos

The chasm of paradox yawns below
I panic on the brink
This God wreaks havoc in my life
He doesn't make sense
He makes a dead child live
Then says 'don't tell'
Gives gifts then wants them back
Is Light, yet the way ahead's all dark
Is Life, yet life must be disowned for him
Is Love to be known, yet out of reach

How huge the gap!
How small my faith!
Lord of contradictions,
Lord of paradox
Lord of truth
Bid me come

He says 'I'll catch you. Come!'
Amen

The Flower

Once, long ago, a silent little seed of minute size was planted in a special garden. It started to sprout in the darkness of its good soil. For a few days when the first shoot of greening popped up there was some excitement. There were tales of marvellous lights and music in the night. But the little plant just seemed to have stem and leaves – green, ordinary – like any other, so for most of its growing time it did not attract too much attention. It was strong and vigorous but not noticeably different.

I had become aware that my struggle somehow opened a Christ-space in my life, like that experienced by Mary Magdalene. There was also the teaching of my Covenant Community that Jesus meets people at their point of need.

In time a bud appeared, and a strange fragrance was noticed by some who came near. Not by everyone, because some were too busy making themselves plastic flower badges to cover the holes in their lives and show that they were right and good. Wafts of the fragrance only came to those without plastic flower badges who knew they weren't good enough, and knew they didn't belong, those aware of something missing from their lives.

The Flower unfolded petal by petal and the news spread among the poor and the sick and the needy and all those with great holes in their lives that to be near the Flower, to breathe its breath, to feast their eyes on its colour and beauty made a big difference. Some said it was like a rose, others thought it a lily, and others again said more like a daisy or a sweet-pea.

It seemed that all who looked on the Flower with honest eyes found their need for beauty and wholeness filled, and they rejoiced to have the life-giving Flower among them. But even some of these became possessive and wanted to build a fence around the Flower so that they alone could have the constant enjoyment of its colour and perfume.

The men with the plastic rightness badges looked at their flowers and at the Flower. They were clever enough to see that there was a difference. If they chose to love the Flower they would have to throw away the rightness badges that covered up their holes because the two sorts of flower couldn't both be true. If they had looked closely at the Flower and breathed deeply enough of what it had to say, they would have been able to love the real one and throw their imitations away. But they didn't so they couldn't. They got very angry about so many people being excited about the Flower. Those who came close to it seemed to carry away some of the beauty and perfume with them when they went home. People could tell where they had been – they were somehow different.

Eventually the plastic badge men got so angry that they decided to destroy the Flower. They pulled it up by the roots, and they jumped on it and ground its shining petals into the mud with their boots. Then they sprayed canned air-freshener around to get rid of the last traces of perfume. Finally they were satisfied that the Flower would cause no more problems and that their badges would again be unchallenged. Only one man felt uneasy – as he looked back at the crushed stem, he thought he saw a drop of blood well up and trickle to the ground. He closed his eyes, then looked again. This time he saw a clear crystal tear drop. 'What rubbish!' he told himself, 'all plants have sap.' So checking that his badge was firmly in place he strode off, telling himself not to be silly.

The people who had loved the Flower were very sad. They tried to remember its fragrance, but that was very hard when all that remained was a stain of colour in the mud. They cried and some of them wondered whether they would have been better off with plastic flowers after all – it would have saved a lot of trouble!

But very soon a woman who had loved the Flower and had too many holes in her life to even try a plastic badge, had an amazing surprise. The Flower was beside her – quite suddenly it was there, even more beautiful than she had remembered. The reds, blues and purples of its petals seemed to be shot through with silver and gold. The fragrance was richer and more precious than ever, and the Flower was present in a mysterious new way that no longer needed roots in the ground. She ran to tell the others, and soon they too saw with their own eyes the Flower, restored, whole, perfect and vibrantly alive. Once again they feasted their eyes on its beauty and breathed its breath of love.

In time they realised that with the destruction of the Flower millions of seeds had been shot into the world – one for every single person. Those who still trust the flower badges which need no tending or watering are still without fragrance or living colour. But those who let the seed grow in the holes in their lives and tend it with love and careful attention find the Flower blossoming within them. Then they too can give joy to those around them, and the healing fragrance of the Flower in their lives goes out from them. Some of them still get trampled by the plastic badge people – then seeds shoot out again to find new heart-spaces to grow in. The Flower will never die again, nor will those in whose lives it grows and blooms.

Betrayal

I was in pain
Help from you to make it go away
Perhaps, but trusting a risk
Take it!
Unconditional love on offer
How could I resist?
The pain – you'd kiss it better!
But the embrace became a serpent coil
Around my body heart and mind
Crushing paralysing eating me up
Until the last pain was worse
Than the first
And then you went away

I began to see that
the responsibility for
providing safe counselling
lay with the professional
concerned, and that
something very wrong
had happened despite my
best efforts to keep the
relationship on track.

Clay

I feel like clay
Not the pristine chunk taken from the block
With the excitement of beginning
But a worked-over puttied mass
Thrown back on the wheel
With the splat of exasperation.
Life seemed for a while
To be shaping up quite well –
There was the base, a little too solid
But providing excellent stability,
The stem refined, compressed and narrowed
By the pressure of pain's fingers,
And then a widening an opening out
A goblet to be filled with love
For pouring out.
And now nothing.
No shape. No direction.
I believe in the Potter –
But still have the urge to be doing something,
Though I don't know what.
Still clay must still wait
Still point at the centre of the turning wheel –
or does it even turn?
I believe in the Potter.

Be still and know that I am God.

Then the
depression set in.
It was an effort to
believe God still
existed – 'finger-
nails faith' I
heard it called.

Listening

I offer you the table of my full attention
Spread with fine linen of love
So that you may lay out the treasures
Of your pain and joy and fear and hope.
Together we will hold and sift them,
Wonder at the state of being human,
Discover in God's reverence for your freedom
The seed of power to grow again
And flower.
Thank you!

But I was still
aware of my own
ability to be there
for others, and of
what being truly
listened to can
accomplish.

Time

I'd been waiting a while
– nearly through to the front –
Fear of the saying, but hope for the cure.
Desperate last try to be rid of disease,
The bane of my life for years and years –
Those who'd tried to help just made it worse –
Nearly my turn!

Through the crowd there pushed
a pleading man –
Please come with me, come now,
Come touch my daughter, she's so ill.
And Jesus went with him.

Faltering hope as off they strode
Then – I matter too! – determination.
To catch up took all remaining strength.
All it needed was to touch his robe,
Quietly, discreetly – that would be enough –
Not keep him from that child.
More life for her still lay ahead,
So hers the greater need.
He was, at last, within my reach –
Hand outstretched I touched his robe
And as power surged from him through me
The cure came.

Initially this piece
was written simply
as a gospel reflection.
It was some years
before I recognised
its relevance to my
own journey, and
even longer before
I could speak of my
wound openly.

Transfixed and overwhelmed I stood
Expecting to be swallowed up then left behind
By the surging crowd.
Go your way, Lord, to the child's sick bed,
And from the depths of my being I thank you
For this cure.

Horror then as he wheeled around
And said 'Who touched me?'
Concern then for that poor father
Keep going – don't mind me.

Who was it?
A silent crowd.
Who was it? Don't be afraid.

So I owned up.
Now go on, go on to the child!
Soon, but I need to hear your story.

To speak of my uncleanness, wounded womanhood?
In front of all these strangers?
All of it? All of it!

So in the tent created by his loving gaze
I told him.
All of it.

With the telling dropped the burden of the years.
Maybe kindling hope in some less brash than me.
Panic then as news came of the daughter's death.
What have you done! Why did you delay?
But on he strode with hope and purpose.

And as I waited in their yard among the wailing friends
I saw with the eyes of my new wholeness
Love that had power even over death.
I waited to see her walk again and talk,
Waited to embrace her
And to share with her the joy of being woman
Healed.

He had time for us both.

Luke 8:40-56

Presence

Where are you, God?
And then the words
Words within and words without –
I am here

A resonance that permeates, pervades
A whisper echoing through the universe
A song in the depths of my being
I am here

Words of love, words of joy
Consoling words, creation words
Nowhere unspoken
I am here

Burning bush that startles
Fine edged sword that knows
No boundaries of skin or heart
I am here

Glimpse of simple sentence
Stretched through time
Reassurance of sustaining
I am here

Effervescent words, ineluctable words
Indwelling, inebriating words
Silent words, dancing words
I am here

And I caught up in the dance
Am present to the All in all

A friend was
dying. I shouted
my protest – and
was astounded,
chastened and
reassured by the
response, a visual
feast of three simple
words moving
through all that is.

In Deep

1993

I was paranoid about edges. I am still paranoid about edges. Why in heaven's name had I got myself into the predicament of volunteering to be lowered over the edge of a 100-metre hole – like 52 stories worth of hole! It all started when I saw the entries in the 1991 Tourism Awards, and there was an attention-grabbing folio from Lost World. I thought I knew my country fairly well, but this was new to me. A leaflet showed a man in a position of exultation on a tall rock against an unearthly golden light streaming through a hole far above. Something sparked deep inside me. Only later did I notice the minute human spider descending its filament in the distance, and realise that this meant going over an edge!

> This article was written about a year after the expedition described. I'd had no idea the venture would be either an ordeal or a spiritual experience! I was just doing it because I had to!

What is this crazy urge about? Nearest I can get is that it is a metaphor for prayer. Glory of encounter with the Ground of our Being. Going deep.

Participants should be moderately fit, they said. The response to my enquiry about what precisely that meant was that if you can handle a half-day's bush walk, you'll be okay. That sounded within my capability. The swimming bits would be fine. What about the money? The $345 was beyond my normal means, but I was becoming aware of the importance of following a dream. A few days after Christmas 1991 I committed myself to the venture. That same day a belated, unforeseeable Christmas card arrived – and enclosed was $100!

Don't know what this is all about, Lord, but here I come.

I picked a date at the end of February and organised a bed at a friend's home in Te Kuiti for the Friday and Sunday nights. My previous abseiling experience was one trip down the four-metre crib wall of a Wellington garden, but they did say full instruction would be given on the day before the big descent…. Didn't tell too many people where I was going in case I bonged out at the last minute. Why? and Who with? were the usual responses. On my own and because I have to, was the best I could do. No prophets of doom, for which I was grateful.

So we gathered at the Waitomo Museum at midday on the Saturday, a motley international crew. Pam from Germany, Aniel from Hawaii, Darcey and Sharon from Australia, Catherine from England, myself the only Kiwi, and the youngest was Geoff from Canada, who in the first five minutes informed us that he'd just come from competing in the Iron Man competition in Auckland! Felt a strong urge to go home! And our guides, Don and Noodles. Age-wise I could have been mother to six of them. We rode in a van to the practice site, picnicked, learnt the basic rules (don't stand on the rope, don't undo first safety belt clip until second one attached), viewed a tomo – a great yawning black hole, and practised abseiling down a 'little' 23-metre drop. I had trouble with my harness, because, as Noodles politely put it, of the position of my centre of gravity! With some engineering ingenuity he finally rigged up a system that attached the upper half of me to the rope as well and so prevented the rather terrifying keeling over backwards. No matter that I looked and felt like a trussed chook. It worked! Recuperative free drinks were made available after the session. Condition: arrival on the pub verandah by flying fox (long and fast), take-off from edge of a cliff, to the cheers of assembled spectators. A stag roared somewhere nearby. 'He fell off yesterday,' said Don cheerfully, 'we haven't found him yet.'

If I can survive that, I can survive anything.

Sunday came. I hadn't slept very well. No reflection on the comfort of the bed in the back-packers' hostel. We were picked up by van and taken to the site of our adventure. We were equipped with wetsuits, helmets with lights, and the batteries which seemed to weigh a ton. Felt like a walrus, and the 'half-day bush walk' suddenly seemed a lot less of a breeze. Short walk to the waiting place at the entrance to our hole. Descent was to be in pairs, and Noodles announced he would go last with me. Don had gone down first to hold the ropes at the bottom. As we chatted to ease the waiting – it took about 15 minutes for each pair to make their descent – I discovered Aniel was a doctor, and what's more an emergency and trauma specialist. He saw my face light up and added 'but I'm used to a high-tech theatre and support staff, so it wouldn't be a lot of use down there.' Never mind! Spent a few minutes identifying the strange sensation in my stomach. Solution: it was like just beginning in labour, when there's nowhere to go but the other end of it. A pleasant diversion was tracking a wonderful aroma to a sun-baked patch of wild mint. Then – time to go. Down onto a very small rock ledge. Safety clips in place. Didn't look over – that would not have helped. Watched Aniel and mate being fastened on to the rope, lean back at a horrific angle into space then disappear. Too soon the call that they had arrived, and it was our turn.

Why am I trusting my life to this young man and his fragile looking gear. What if the rope breaks? What if I panic half way? Perfect trust casts out fear. Fear is counter-productive. They haven't lost anyone yet – why should they start with me? Trusting is the best option. Is this what faith is about? Entrusting one's whole being to a God who knows that it's all under control. Focus on absolute obedience for this bit. Put your right foot here, your left foot there, lean back against my hand. Walk down to that rock. Mind your knee. Now we're on the way. Faith accomplishes the impossible!

The descent was fascinating, down a chasm lined with creepers and ferns. Feeding the rope into the rack was surprisingly hard work. Harness worked well and Noodles chatted reassuringly. He took photos with my camera – later useful evidence that it had not all been a dream. Twenty metres from the bottom he announced he was going ahead and I could do the last bit alone. Panic stations!

Lord, is this what happens when you disappear from view?

Finally hit the bottom and despite the sense of triumph it was a few minutes before my legs felt normal. That was the easy bit, said Noodles. Big welcome from the others, then a wonderful lunch of filled rolls and cake. An awesome place, like a cathedral, light streaming through the rose window, the hole so far above us. I was impressed by the guides' reverence for the place and its fragile ecology – we were told not to stand on the plants as regeneration takes much longer at that depth.

Want time to explore, savour, and worship in this extraordinary place, but the others are all ready to move off.

If I had known then what I know now, I'd have known it was totally impossible for me to do what I did in the next five hours. Even without all the extra weight of the gear. We were to go upstream through the cave system until we met daylight. Hours filled to overflowing with water, rocks, drama, exhaustion, splendour, more exhaustion, respites, sheer terror, yet more exhaustion and absolute awe. There were golden stalactites and stalagmites, fossilised giant oysters 25 million years old with the pearls still in them. There were rocks of every imaginable size, shape and texture to be gone over, round, between. There was the rock in the photo which had initially captured my imagination. They called it the Jesus rock.

So they can feel it too!

And the water varied from ankle-deep to waist-deep to bottomless. Swimming was pleasantly cooling and wet-suits gave buoyancy. Getting out, when gravity struck, was another matter altogether. Water that was by turns rushing, gentle, foaming, trickling, roaring, seething. Then there was water in a deep, black pool at the base of a waterfall – and an invitation to jump from a five-metre cliff into it. We had arrived at the edge of the pool. The way to the jumping off point was up a flimsy-looking ladder with finger-thick rungs and slender wire sides. It hung close to the cliff-face, too close to gain an easy toehold. I watched fascinated as the volunteer jumpers used a knee to push off from the wall, enough to get a foothold on the next rung. 'Not for me, this bit,' I told Don. 'Sorry,' he said, 'that's the way out!' So up I went. Rationale rapidly changed to – if I jump I'll have to climb that thing again. So I lay awhile on a ledge at the top recovering breath, happily listening to the others shrieking as they plunged into the darkness to the pool below. Then I was human enough not to mind too much when one of the young women, despite 15 minutes of patient encouragement while standing on the brink, just could not bring herself to jump. Only trouble was I'd watched her struggle and felt every twinge of every emotion with her, so I was a bit of a wreck when we moved on again.

Jumping off into the darkness takes another kind of faith again. Lord, you never force us. Our choices are our own.

By this stage I was feeling like a very weary, elderly walrus and the others still had gazelle-like energy. I was left behind the group time after time, though someone was always at hand. I realised that visibility was much reduced when travelling away from the others, which added to my difficulty in making progress.

Is that what church is about – sharing our little lights with each other, to throw a combined light on the path ahead?

So often I said 'I can't' when a rock loomed with no apparent handholds, or I faced a span that was too wide for me to be confident that I wouldn't wrench a knee on landing. The response was always the same: you have to. So I did. As I wrote to the guides later, I may not have held the record for the oldest (that stood at 71) or heaviest (160 kilos), but I'm sure I said 'I can't' the oftenest! At least all the ceilings were high and there was no need to wriggle through small spaces. That had been checked out as part of my feasibility study. They had talked to us about eels and spiders, not much of a problem to me when we were up in the sunlight. Even less of one now when the main concern was how to pick up each foot (sometimes quite literally!) to put it in front of the other, and hope the putting down place did not wobble and wasn't slippery.

Dear God, get me out of here alive!

The one place Dan and Noodles described as dangerous was a narrow stretch of white water containing a whirlpool. Cheerfully they said if we went down there they would not be able to get us back! So please to follow instructions exactly. We were to step precisely where shown, and that included using Noodles' braced thigh as a step to get from one side to the safety of a ledge on the other.

I'm too heavy. More obedience. Is this what receiving support means? It's so hard to walk on someone, even when they are inviting or rather commanding you to. Don't argue, it's the only way through. Is this laying down your life for others?

And then a blessed rest on a plateau towards the end. My rests were always shorter that everyone else's because I was always the last to arrive. This was a real break. We passed around a cup of hot, sweet lemon-tea, then turned our lights out. Gradually we saw a starry splendour of glow-worms and sat in silent awe for a long time.

God, is this a taste of heaven? Tears of relief and gratitude for beauty, silence, being still. Communion of the shared cup and shared struggle to get here, but there's no way we could claim to have earned such a moment. It's a gift.

The struggle to survive and keep moving resumed. It couldn't be much longer, we'd been going four hours already. I was exhausted beyond anything I had ever experienced and fell heavily banging my knee on – inevitably – a rock. No time to stop. Geoff, the iron man, became my tow truck, support and knight in shining armour. A glimpse of daylight, a precious, unbelievably precious relief. Exultation – we've done it! Acknowledgement of the guardians of the cave, two silhouetted faces formed of rock and trees. Dismay as we emerged into sunlight and were confronted with a 20-metre stream-bank to climb. Without Geoff I'd never have made it. Then a long, long walk back across the paddocks to the hut.

These young people are so good half-carrying me like this. I wouldn't have come if I thought I'd need so much help. I'm not used to imposing on people. It would be embarrassing if I had the energy left to be embarrassed. Just accept it. And Noodles offering to take my battery pack. Jesus, you offer to take my burdens – how often do I accept the offer? You let Simon of Cyrene help you with yours when your strength had run out. You know what it's like being the needy one.

Banana-peeling boots and wetsuits left us with sensations of astonishing weightlessness. Barbecued sausages and the rest of the lemon-tea were restorative. We swapped addresses and congratulated each other on becoming part of the select group – less than 1000 worldwide – who have experienced this incredible adventure to the centre of the earth.

The longest journey surely is within. I have accomplished the impossible, but only with the enabling skills of the guides and the support and care of the group who became 'church for a day' for me and each other. We have truly been 'in deep'.

Waikanae

I

Walking on wet sky between sea and surf
With shimmer and shadow of a shimmer
Quilting ruching overlaying patterned sand

I breathe again

Stripped clean bones hand finger foot and wing
Knobbled arms and legs on dry wind
fingered ripples
Huge thighs and spines and antlered skulls

Of prehistoric beasts

Lace frills left behind to fly apart
Bubbles windsurf while the wetness lasts
As the same gust sizzles storms of stinging sand

Round land-ward ankles

Terns ballet gracing air dive arrow straight for fish
Black half unfurled umbrella flaps its cormorant wings
Pied stilt on long three-knee'd reflected legs

Dances with ease

II

Dear God so many ways you show yourself
On a beach
Power and thunder ripple caress
Ever changing ever unchanged
Meeting inviting mingling drawing
The river to join sea's self
So God draw me
To you

On a dune
With seaweed shells shaped wood
I build an altar
To the meeting of the waters
And worship

Waikanae beach
does wonders
for my soul. I
was staying with
Christian friends
who lived nearby,
and summed
up my littoral
reflections as a
thank-you gift.

Cave

It's lonely in the cave
Lonely
But safe
In the dark
With my back to the wall
Where only the very brave dare visit
The last tentative venture out
Coaxed by promise of care
Brought joy at first
Then storm chaos
And all-consuming pain
Back to the back
The very back
Of the cave
I set before you life and death
'Choose life' says God
To take that risk again
Can only be done without hope
Only with a fearful readiness
To be surprised
Invitation of a disembodied hand
Brought disbelief
And gratitude
And with acceptance
Blind panic
Choosing life
Means dying
A thousand deaths
Knowing the destination
Is resurrection
The back of the cave
Was safe
Very safe
But lonely

Functioning okay
on the outside,
but inside…

The Invitation

The following three pieces were my entry for the 1993 London Tablet John Harriott Memorial Award for religious journalism. It was my wonderful mother-in-law's idea: she thought I could do it. The task sounded relatively easy: three 800-word pieces on anything religious. But I was astounded to be placed third out of a worldwide field.

She had prepared her own funeral liturgy. I knew that because she'd asked for resource material over a year previously. So we hunted for it and came across the notebook with the instructions, hymns, readings and prayers, all neatly set down. That made it so much easier. She was the only Christian, the only Catholic in her family, and had wanted to simplify matters for both them and for the parish. Not that many people in the parish knew her – she had been virtually housebound since before her baptism into her Lord. Severe arthritis, particularly bad in her ankles, a blood condition, the ravages of physical and emotional pain had all, day by long day, been taking their toll for many years.

I took her communion each week and had grown to love her for her gentleness, lack of self-pity and her grateful response to even the smallest kindness, not to mention the caring welcome she always gave me. And her faith, which was vibrant.

One day I arrived with her weekly Portion, and as usual asked her what reading she had chosen. Favourites were the promises in Revelations 21 of the new life where the tears would be wiped away, and there would be no more death, mourning or sadness; the poetry in Job 38 and 39 describing the magnificence of creation, and the 23rd Psalm. This day it was to be something different: 2 Samuel 9. Not a familiar reference. I must have looked slightly quizzical. Yes, she said, there is a story.

During the night she had dreamed of seeing herself seated in her room reading her Bible. In the morning she had no memory of what she had read, simply the picture. But there was a reference in her mind to 2 Samuel 9. It meant as little to her as it did to me. So she had picked up the Scriptures and read a story from 3000 years ago that reached through the centuries to have an extraordinary impact on her – and on me, too.

What she read was this: King David asked whether there was anyone left of Saul's family so that he could show kindness for his friend Jonathan's sake. Ziba, one of Saul's old servants, was summoned and David asked the question of him whether there was anyone left of Saul's family so that he could show him God's kindness. There is still one of Jonathan's sons, said Ziba, Meribaal who is a man with crippled feet. So Meribaal was sent for and came humbly into the king's presence. David welcomed him, restored to him the lands and property that had been Saul's, and said that he was welcome always to eat at the royal table. Meribaal was overcome by his unworthiness for all this but accepted the invitation. David entrusted Ziba with the overseeing of his affairs and harvesting the produce from the newly returned land. So, concludes the story, Meribaal ate at David's table like one of the king's sons. He lived in Jerusalem since he always ate at the king's table. And he had crippled feet.

She was amazed that this should so accurately speak of her own predicament – the same as Meribaal's, the crippled feet. The writer by his repetition of the phrase (verses 4 and 13) leaves no doubt that he too saw some significance in this. She felt a great awe that God should have acknowledged her personally, should have reached into her spirit to draw her attention to the previously unseen story, and should have given her this unmistakable invitation to his table. She accepted the invitation with joy. The King wanted her, really wanted her to dine with him at his table.

We read the story again together and as we shared the Eucharist that morning our hearts sang with the angels. We were both caught up in the presence of the Host who with such tenderness and in this unmistakable way had communicated his loving desire to share this Meal with her, to make provision for her future. What privilege!

The memory of this event became part of all the other Eucharists we celebrated. In earthly terms her situation did not change – poverty, pain and family turbulence continued. But her centre was calm and confident that the promises of Scripture would be even more completely fulfilled after death. Her illness became acute but she was not expected to die. It happened anyway, quietly and without fuss, and so we found her notebook.

At the funeral mass, a predominantly non-Christian gathering in our parish church, we were able to tell the story of her dream, the story of Meribaal, which became her own story; the story of a God who continues to take the initiative in communicating with us, who uses his Living Word to speak now-words that transform hearts and lives. We told of the words that encouraged, engendered trust and hope in a future free from the pain, sadness and mourning. We celebrated the provision of the Food for our present journey, and the King's personal invitation to our friend to life in the new Jerusalem. He had truly called her to his banqueting table – and she had accepted the invitation.

An Intrinsic Moral Evil?

'Put a smile on your face and keep it there while I tell you I'm pregnant.' To his eternal credit my doctor did just that. Nor did he mention the possibility of an abortion. But he did make a prompt referral to a specialist! It was my tenth pregnancy. Five children, three miscarriages and an ectopic pregnancy; and with the previous baby I'd had blood pressure problems, and an emergency caesarean after an eclamptic fit, with its possibilities of cerebral haemorrhage and kidney damage.

This piece was prompted by Pope John Paul II's 1993 description of contraception as an 'intrinsic moral evil.' By then I knew that reflecting on my own lived experience constituted theology – so I did that, drawing on the events of 1979-80. It was published in *The Tablet* (London) with the less contentious title of 'Mother and Child.'

I knew in faith that God must know where we were at. This new pregnancy had occurred during careful use of Natural Family Planning. But what exactly did He want me/us to do about the situation? I had no thought of not continuing the pregnancy, despite the edict from the hospital: you do realise, don't you, that we can't promise you a live baby? Yes, I realised all right. And also that while they tactfully didn't spell it out, and they would do their best, they couldn't actually guarantee that I would survive, either.

Where was God in all this? Very present in all sorts of ways, but not providing any obvious answers. Normally I don't have ready repartee, so recognised as a gift the comment I heard myself making in response to an ecological friend who asked 'And was it planned?' 'Yes,' I said, 'it just wasn't us who did the planning!' It was my faith that there is a Higher Authority than the doctor's that kept me from going up the wall with worry, thus precipitating the blood pressure problem again. I just had to keep calm!

While we discussed the situation as a couple, ultimately solutions were going to be my responsibility. We had read and taken on board Humanae Vitae, but were now having to reassess our understanding in the light of this particular set of circumstances. I did not want to be 'let off' as an extreme case – that always seemed a patronising, demeaning permission to give God second best. I had a real conviction that there was a positive God-intended path for us to follow. The discernment process to discover this involved prayer, study and consultation with our parish priest.

It's only recently that I have acquired the language to recognise that this baby was teaching us theology in those months before his birth. We were examining our experience in the light of tradition, culture and revelation within the context of our relationship with a loving God. It was indeed our 'faith seeking understanding.'

What became clear was that the church appears to deal with the moral question of contraception in its 'pure' form, in isolation from any other considerations. It seems to ignore the fact that the question can only arise within the complex web of a family relationship. Contraception just cannot be considered in isolation from the circumstances of the individual family. There is an acknowledgement of a hierarchy of truths within the body of Christian teaching – some are more central than others. Surely within a pastoral situation there is also a hierarchy of considerations that must be allowed to interplay and shed light on each other. Can we have any faith that God is a God of commonsense?

There were profound considerations of justice. What was justice for my other five children? I was risking their mother's life going through with this pregnancy; another would be foolhardy. What was justice for my husband, already unwell with a condition which claimed his life a few years later? Was it just to risk leaving him as the sole parent of five or six young children? What was justice for my family and friends who coped admirably during my months in hospital before the last baby and again before this one? Should they have to go through that again? Or even – dare I say it – what was justice for myself? Coping with a large family was okay in a non-pregnant state but I had a feeling that there was something intrinsically morally wrong with putting my God-given life at risk; and what did my basic dignity as a daughter of God imply? All these factors needed to be allowed to interact with the 'absolute' that contraception is 'always' wrong. While finances were stretched, that was not a major consideration. Simply wanting to stay alive surely did not constitute selfishness.

Something had to be done. The question then became how. The pill was medically inadvisable. Total abstinence was seriously considered (what does God really want?) but was not a viable proposition. Ultimately, I had a tubal ligation during the elective caesarian delivery of a healthy baby boy. My recovery was uneventful. God had faithfully brought us unscathed through those roaring fires and deep waters. And had given us clear indication that his path for us lay in actively avoiding such places in the future. During our time of discernment, a concerned acquaintance assured me that God 'never' willed contraception. I beg to differ.

Humility and Me

As a somewhat scrupulous teenager I had terrible trouble with humility. I would examine myself for signs of this most prized virtue, then writhe in agonies of frustration when having found a trace of it I fell into the trap of self-congratulation. 'Hey, wow, I'm being humble.' And ipso facto I had shot myself, humility and all, in the foot!

The previous two pieces were current issues for me in 1993. For the piece below I drew on the context of an earlier Pentecost retreat moment.

In my thirties I embraced with enormous relief the concept that all goodness is God's gift to us. That relieved me of the responsibility of claiming any credit for anything that was going at all well in my life. It was simply the59 Lord's doing. There was nothing more to be said. During those years, how much genuinely offered affirmation I rejected by redirecting it to God. Not known at this address! Try Heaven! I was simply the servant doing my duty. I kept hearing perceptive people trying to tell me this might have something to do with lack of self-esteem. Which didn't make a lot of sense. I even heard the suggestion that putting energy into loving myself the way I loved my neighbour might be useful for growth. Huh?

But on the other hand there was an internal, very private arrogance which completely blocked any vision of myself as a sinner. After all, I had never committed adultery, or robbed a bank or even simply refused to cook the dinner. I did what was expected of me. My best friend in the third-form had told me I was smug. By now it was called self-righteousness, even if I declined overtly to take the credit for any particular action. What do you do to get rid of self-righteousness? I asked various priests at retreats. I didn't ever receive an answer I understood.

Eventually the time came. It was during an eight-day directed retreat. It was Pentecost Sunday. The Scripture I was given was the story in Luke 7 of the woman who was a sinner. As I read it I became aware of my profound jealousy of the woman who had sinned so much that she was able to repent in this enormously deep and dramatic way.

I knew Jesus was responding to her, valuing her in a way that was out of my reach – because I wasn't a sinner. But then again that made me like Simon and the other Pharisees in the story. God help me! That wasn't right either! Jesus was not too keen on them, nor on their associate who thanked God he was not a sinner like the fellow at the back of the

Temple. I definitely did not want to be identified with the Pharisees. I could see by then that I actually wanted a seat among the sinners. There was even one with my name on it but I was quite unable to reach it, let alone sit in it! I wanted to be able to repent like that woman and receive that sort of love and understanding from Jesus. Maybe if I went out and had a good old sinful rampage? Perhaps not the ideal solution!

So I tried another tack. I had memories of Sister Mary Angela, or was it Marie Therese, telling us at primary school that the sins, the personal sins of each individual had made some difference to the pain of the crucifixion. Okay, Lord, this feels like being stuck in concrete, I can't move. This is (gulp) my sin of self-righteousness. What did it do to you? How can you help me shift it?

And then it happened. I saw in the distance a hill with three crosses on it, but the gentlest Voice was right beside me: 'Your self-righteousness has been the nails that have held my hands and feet fixed to the wood, when I wanted to walk through your life to touch and heal.'

The sheer horror at having blocked that healing love, at the arrogance that had privately assured me I was okay at that moment exploded like dynamite in my consciousness and blasted the concrete of my self-righteousness to smithereens. Then the tears came. Tears of repentance for struggling with this thing in my own strength. Tears of recognition that I was truly a sinner just like the rest of the human race. Tears of gratitude and joy for this gift of new sight and understanding. For several days I was quite high on the fact that I was a sinner, and what's more I was always going to be a sinner.

There are always going to be new corners of darkness discovered, into which I can invite the healing touch of Jesus. There are always going to be the acts and attitudes of unlove towards myself and others. What a cause for rejoicing! Repentance and forgiveness were mine at last.

I used to be self-righteous, but now I'm ... what? A joyful sinner, too deeply grateful for the gift of clear sight to want to put any other labels on. I was blind, and now I see! Becoming whole is the task of a lifetime. Alleluia!

Humility? My picture is of a child dancing with a butterfly settled on her hair. Any effort to capture it, or even to ascertain that it is still there will cause it to fly away – and will certainly interrupt the dance.

Mending

Eyes wide with panic she gazed into the blackness and fought
to steady her breathing. Tentatively she stretched a hand into
the bed-space beside her. It was empty. Thank God, it was
empty. It had been a nightmare. He hadn't really come back.
As she struggled to sift dream from reality, the events of the last
six months came into focus. He was dead, killed in an accident
while drunk driving. Fortunately no-one else was hurt. They
had come to tell her quietly and sympathetically. The shock
was profound, but easier to deal with than the feelings that
had followed in a wild whirl in the weeks and months since
then. Somewhere she had heard that where a relationship has been a complex of love and
hate then grieving is correspondingly complex. At least that information had stopped her
thinking she had gone mad.

This 'story' was
published under
a pseudonym. A
few details were
fictionalised, but
the experiences
were real.

There had been all the sympathy and tragic faces when she had felt like singing alleluias at
the top of her voice. There had been the other widows at church soothing gently. 'Dear,
I know just how you feel.' Like hell they did! There had been the hundreds of cards and
letters about such a fine man, generous, proud of his family, a wonderful Catholic father.
Her experience had been so different from that – the drinking, the verbal and emotional
violence, economic violence, physical violence on occasion too. She had struggled to
reconcile marriage vows of fidelity during sickness and bad times, with providing the
children and herself with a sane and healthy environment. It couldn't have gone on much
longer anyway, she mused. Consciously counteracting the nightmare of his coming back
she spread-eagled across the entire bed. It was hers now, a safe place. She was no longer
apprehensive about going there, being there ….

It was all inside out and back to front. She didn't miss him at all, but the pain of not
missing him was intense, the pain and sadness of a transition that was too easy, the pain
of being able to discard sixteen years of marriage with such relief.

Five years later, on retreat, she rebelled at dealing yet again with 'that old stuff.' 'I've done
it so often, I'm sick of it.' 'But if that's what is coming up for you, there is more to do.'
She had steadfastly refused to relate to her dead husband. She presumed he was forgiven,
in heaven, enjoying God's peace and love. Which was okay. No problems with that. She'd
simply been getting on with her own life, quite well really. The children had settled down
eventually and were growing up in a peaceful home. No need to bring him into it at all.
Yet here she was with the director, suggesting meeting him in prayer, with Jesus there just
for her, to support her and accept whatever she would be feeling.

'I don't want to. But I suppose I could give it a go.'

She imagined a strong comforting Jesus who assured her that the meeting would go at her
pace and she didn't have to force herself to do anything she wasn't ready for. He would
not leave her and would understand whatever happened. They set off hand in hand to the
meeting place, and stopped by a high wall. She knew her husband was on the other side

of it and that the wall was going to come down. She couldn't look, and buried her face in Jesus' tunic. He put his arms round her and waited. The wall crumbled behind her. The panic of the nightmare seized her again, and lasted, and lasted. Interminably. No-one rushed her. It was okay to be terribly afraid. Jesus and her husband were talking quietly to each other. 'She is really hurting and scared.' 'We'll have to be very patient.' 'There's plenty of time now.' And they waited. And waited.

Clinging to Jesus she was aware of an extraordinary unsuspected anger rising from her depths, and before she could stop it a great scream came out – 'You deserve to rot in hell!' She was utterly shocked – it was the most terrible thing she'd ever said in her life, and with Jesus' arms around her too! Where was her forgiveness and generosity? Jesus didn't even flinch. There was a silence. Then her husband with a gentleness she had never heard before said, 'Yes, I know, and part of me is doing just that until you release me.'

Eventually Jesus whispered to her, 'We can share the Eucharist when you are ready.' 'I'm ready.' So together the three of them kneaded the dough of all their suffering and baked it in the fire of Love. The wine had all their fears and anger dissolved in it. As they waited for the meal to be ready, Jesus washed their feet. Then her husband washed her feet and Jesus' feet. She moved to get up to take her turn to do the washing, feeling strangely lightened. But her husband, with the same new gentleness said: 'There's no need for you to do it now – you were washing our feet during all those years of our marriage.'

The bread was ready, so it was blessed and broken and shared. As they shared the cup, for the first time she was able to look her husband in the face. She saw nothing but love. She wept.

Later on, while trying to convey something of the enormity of this experience to her director, she said, 'I feel so exhausted and weak and fragile – like I've just had heart surgery.' 'Yes,' smiled the retreat director gently, 'you have had heart surgery!'

Straightening

Bent double I was, with the weight
The weight of the trouble
The trouble of the secret, the old secret
The dark and dreadful secret.
I saw no sun or sky but only the distorted shadow
Of a crippled frame.
I saw a sunless world of feet and dust and dung
No caring face, no tree, no hill.
My weight held up by props
I saw my pained and plodding feet
Watching always watching
Where to put them
Watchful and wary where and how to tread
In case I let the secret
The clawing consuming secret
Out to rampage in the world.

Then drawn by the call of a Beautiful Voice
I came to the One of the Beautiful Feet.
So I could see his face he knelt
And whispering said what's heavy and dark
Becomes light when brought into the light.
With his ear so close, so lovingly close
It was at last no longer hard
To say what had to be said.
He touched me, a long, long touch.
And with the touch came backbone
Came the lightening, the straightening
Courage to speak my truth
To shout and sing
To look folks in the eye
To throw away the props,
Begin to learn to dance,
And in the colours of the world
To know relief and rediscover joy.

By 1994 I was doing some letter-counselling, and a young woman had acknowledged childhood sexual abuse. I was praying for her and asked Jesus, 'Did you minister to women who had been abused like that?' The response: 'Do you remember the woman bent double?' I read that story again with new eyes, then the poem wrote itself. Later I saw this too was about my own story, but not at the time.

Luke 13:10-11

A Tiger Named Susanna

'The Master would say … the shortest distance between a human being and Truth is a story.'[4]

Stories, even biblical stories, are mythological and inherently imaginative in that they point to much more than meets the eye; they are out to elicit a response from both head and heart … they are meant to provide us with images and ways of thinking about life's imponderables with God as the reference point.'[5]

The following case history is an example of the power of a story from the Hebrew Scriptures in a woman client's journey to liberation and wholeness. She has given me permission to use her story because of the present importance seen in the community and the church of bringing into the light the issue of sexual abuse by members of the clergy, counsellors and other professionals.[6] By letting her story be told she is now able to acknowledge God's role in the healing process, and affirm her own transition from victim to survivor.

This assignment for an Old Testament Women course I was doing as part of the Diploma in Pastoral Ministry, felt very scary, as 'J' stood for 'I'! But it was empowering to have begun understanding big pictures and structural patterns, and that some people were doing something about sexual abuse by clergy. I was almost ready to begin redeeming the experience by working for change myself.

J had been struggling for some years with the damaging effects of an unethical relationship with a minister of religion to whom she had gone for counselling. He was a well-known person with a position of responsibility in his church, and she had been too afraid of the effects on him of revealing to anyone the extent of her distress and depression to be able to do so. She eventually decided that this state of affairs could not continue so sought further counselling, at which for the first time she named her abuser. During that session J described her emotional state as being like a ravenous needy tiger behind a blue velvet curtain. A calm exterior, but very dangerous to anyone who came at all close! That counsellor decided the tiger could be a useful symbol and asked J to give it a name. Initially she was puzzled: Anne, Mary or Betsey didn't seem right. The counsellor told her to wait and a name would come. One did. It was Susanna. They also established during that session that as a 5 in Enneagram terms J needed to get in touch with her 8, the animal symbol for which was a tiger![7] Her power, strength and capacity for aggression were waiting to bring her health.

As she returned home she wondered where the name Susanna had sprung from, as she knew no-one of that name. She thought perhaps it could be a biblical name. The concordance referred her to Daniel 13, and for the first time she read the story of the original Susanna:[8]

> A beautiful, virtuous young woman from a respected family used to take a daily walk in her husband's garden once the two elderly judges who were involved in hearing cases at her home had left for the day. These two had each

without admitting it developed a passion for Susanna and had contrived to see her every day. One day, having ostensibly left, they each retraced their steps, came face to face, and having admitted their designs to each other, joined forces. They hid, and spied on her as, planning to have a bathe, she sent her maids away. They immediately propositioned her and resorted to blackmail – if she did not do as they wanted they would give evidence against her of adultery with a non-existent young man. This would result in her being stoned to death. She preferred remaining innocent and in their power to sinning in the eyes of the Lord. So, (matching the classic teaching of modern women's self-defence[9]) 'she cried out as loud as she could.' The men too made a noise, made their accusations and left, with the servants and presumably her husband and family quite aghast as 'nothing of this sort had ever been said of Susanna.' She was brought to trial the next day, and though her heart was confident in God, the word of the two elderly men was believed. Without even being heard she was condemned to death. Again she cried out, this time to the Eternal God who knew her innocence. Then 'The Lord roused the Holy Spirit residing in a boy called Daniel' and in a shout (foreshadowing that of Pilate[10]) he proclaimed his disowning of the verdict of death. On this occasion, the community did take note, and allowed him to obtain separate evidence from the two judges. They were duly convicted by their differing stories, and received the punishment they had intended for Susanna. Her life was spared and the family rejoiced and thanked God that she had been acquitted of anything dishonourable. And of course Daniel's reputation for prophetic wisdom was enhanced.

J was absolutely staggered by the similarities with her own story, and was awed by the way her attention had been drawn to the story. She felt an enormous sense of God's support and understanding, as well as an awakening hope that justice could be done in her case too. It would once again be the word of a woman against that of a powerful man. Two verses in particular had a great impact on her: verse 6 speaks about 'Wickedness coming … through elders and judges posing as guides to the people.'[11] This released in J a great and healthy anger at the hypocrisy of clergy and others engaged in this type of relationship who shelter behind the screen of community respect. The other was verse 57: 'This is how you have been behaving with the daughters of Israel and they were too frightened to resist; but here is a daughter of Judah who could not stomach your wickedness.' This began J's consideration of the possibility of other women, past and future, suffering a similar fate to her own at the hands of the same man.

Another connection that startled J was recalling, after reading the story, a dream she had more than a year previously. She had entered a room where she discovered two of her abuser sitting at a table. Neither of these men had been telling the other what he was doing. J felt thoroughly confused about which of these men to say anything to. This dream had given her a framework in which to understand what was going on at the time – the psychological splitting that occurs in perpetrators: 'This erotic intoxication allows a man to live in two realities: one in which he is being sexually intrusive and another in which the professional disguise can be trotted out at will for protection, disguise and the maintenance in his own mind of a propriety that somewhere inside him he may wish to reclaim.'[12] To see in Susanna's story someone else pursued by two elders who did not let each other know what they were up to confirmed the dream and increased her sense of both being able to identify with the biblical Susanna and also of being led and strengthened by the God of Susanna and Daniel.

The counsellor had suggested that the tiger named Susanna was in need of care, attention and nurture. So over the next couple of years J spent time and energy on feeding the hungry parts of herself. This inner Susanna became less ferocious and frightening, and more of an ally and source of strength.

As J read and reread the Susanna story, the question of 'what if he does the same thing to someone else?' began to loom larger in her consciousness. Eventually she was able to take the risk of laying a complaint with the church, with increasing confidence that this was in the interests of all concerned. Buoyed up by her Susanna experience, she was confident that God would provide her with a Daniel in a situation where she was admittedly the accuser, but she would still be pitting her word against that of a powerful member of the church community. She was unaware that the name Daniel in Hebrew means 'my judge is God,'[13] though that was her faith.

It was a long slow process, and during this time she became considerably more in touch with her own strength and her need to seek justice for herself, as well as the need to require accountability from her abuser, and protection for other women. It was during this period I was able to offer support and treasure the Susanna story with her. Also I encouraged her as she eventually faced the prospect of a mediation conference between herself, the minister concerned and a mediator, at which she was to present her demands for recompense, apology and disciplinary action. Susanna the tiger was very much part of the preparation for the conference. The idea of sitting facing the man who had harmed her was made a lot easier with the awareness of a sleek, protective tiger at her feet. J and a friend had prayed for a Daniel for her case, there was an abundance of wisdom and clarity put at her service. Susanna the tiger and the God of Susanna, innocent biblical victim of sexual abuse, were both present with J at the conference, giving her what she needed. The outcome was largely satisfactory.

Sexual abuse of women by some members of the clergy as they are involved in counselling and pastoral work has recently come into the open as an issue. It takes great courage to take on the task of challenging 'such elders … posing as guides to the people.'
There is an enormous need for the many women damaged by this sort of relationship to be empowered by their own tigers called Susanna, to take courage and speak out, knowing that God is on their side, and that at long last the church is learning to give their pain the attention it deserves. 'A theology of Transformation … expresses righteous anger in the face of evil, giving rise to action and advocacy. It is about God's work of making justice and healing brokenness by celebrating small victories, saying no in unexpected places, breaking the silence on what is deemed secret and taboo, challenging oppressive attitudes which are cast in concrete, standing with those trapped in victimisation and supporting their journeys to healing and safety.'[14] And so stories give birth to new stories…

Waiting

Jesus, your tomb-time is a template of my now
The leaves of time that was have fallen limp
and brown
A lifted autumn bulb inert in death has need of dark
There's waiting time then time to plant in faith
That spring will call forth tiny tips of green
And in time's fullness, flowers

My jigsaw has been pulled apart
The edge and telling pieces gone
What's left I lay upon the table of your love
And wait for pieces soon to come
A new picture to emerge
I mourn the death of what has been
And wait in passionless patience
Bordering on expectancy
For your resurrection and my own

A Holy Saturday
moment – the end
of a difficult phase
without any real
sense of what might
begin.

Tūrangawaewae

1995 – 2005

During these years the last of my children left home. And finally there was space to spend time as I chose on my own needs and the needs of others. Learning and doing theology/thealogy has given me a new slant to questions of how and where my God can be recognised. My own experiences of marginalisation and those of the people among whom I have been a chaplain have brought a realisation that this is truly where the gospel Jesus is at home. I know too that through my own experiences I am 'one with' them – not 'other' or 'better' than.

My inner journey and outer life have become more integrated after a profound and lengthy journey with a psychotherapist of great patience and skill. That has been a sacramental experience in itself. Damage from the hard years has gradually healed, and my 'standing place' made firm. Speaking my own truth has become easier. There is a new abundance of freedom, joy and peace. Any work I do now as a counsellor or spiritual director has a different resonance. The 'In Deep' experience in the caves near Waitomo (see In Deep) became a powerful metaphor for the sacred journey of psychotherapy, as well as for the connection with prayer that I had made at the time.

I have difficulty these days answering the question: 'Are you a Christian?' With all the assumptions a 'yes' would engender, that won't work. Neither does a 'no.' All I can say is that the Jesus of the gospels is the Friend and Brother who is still the closest companion of my Way. Jesus and God have re-shaped themselves in wonderful images. I can understand, though, the many other women who through their life experiences and feminist journeys have needed to leave the institutional church to heal, without being able to connect in a useful way with any evolving God-images. Leaving the church, 'going out into the desert' has proved, contrary to expectation, a fruitful and companionable experience. I honour those whose paths have led close to mine, especially the women of ExAlt and Susanna Group, and those of my time with the Quakers (Religious Society of Friends).

In my writings of the last ten years, I can find hints of Fowler's Stage 5, 'Conjunctive Faith.' This is characterised by 'a capacity to own one's most significant beliefs, while recognising that they are relative, partial and imperfect perceptions of reality.' People in this stage 'are not likely to be true believers in the sense of a dialectical, single-minded, uncritical devotion to a cause or ideology … They know the line between the righteous and the sinners goes through the heart of each of us and our communities, rather than between us and them.'

These days, one of my favourite images of God is as 'Elephant,' specifically the one the blind men fought over in the folk-story,[15] each insisting that his description was the only accurate one! My images of God do not need to threaten or disprove anyone else's! I began to ask what God wanted 'for' me rather than 'from' me. Some earlier important moments are re-visited and integrated with further life experience.

Many good things do still happen in the church, and I rejoice that in some quarters it is now attempting in some measure to face its shadow. For me and for many others, particularly women, this is too little and too late. The energy withdrawn from that arena I now choose to spend mainly on enjoying this beautiful world and nurturing my friendships, and when it seems that I could use knowledge that has accrued for the sake of others who have had similar experiences of abuse and/or alienation, I will do what seems appropriate. God truly is in the other place!

The Wash

'Phew,' sighed Marie as she peeled out of her sticky uniform. It had been a busy day on the ward with several post-operative patients from yesterday's surgery needing large amounts of care and time. She caught sight of herself in the mirror as she reached for a tee-shirt, and instead of hastily looking away as she usually did, she stopped and thoughtfully let her gaze wander up and down her own image. 'Maybe I don't look so bad,' she pondered. 'Could be worse. Better without a few more kilos. Shall I have another go at losing some weight? It just goes back on though, far too easily, after all the enormous effort of losing it. Maybe I am doomed to a lifetime of being fat!

An anonymously published 'story,' with fictional details, incorporating ('embodying') my own post-surgery experience, and revisiting the prayer-experience described in 'Incarnation.'

Could I really feel okay about how I look right now?' She looked with distaste at her hips and thighs, and then with relief at her short blond curls and eyes that were a deep sea-green. Some bits were fine, but the rest…!

Maybe, just maybe, that patient this morning had given her a key to the problem. She and the other student nurse had helped the woman shower as it was her first time up after her hysterectomy. She was fortyish, greying, unremarkable and not exactly sylph-like. But there was a cheerfulness about the way she accepted their help, and a certain peace about her. In the afternoon Marie had gone back to the same woman to do one her patient interviews.

'How are you feeling, Mrs Grant?' She sat down by the bed to ask the next question. 'We need to get some practice doing histories of patients' social background. I was wondering how you'd feel about answering a few questions if you feel up to it?' Mrs Grant smiled, 'Yes, dear, that's all right. You were such a help this morning, so I'd be happy to do that for you.'

Marie ran through the standard questions about age – 43, marital status – divorced, family size – seven, five boys, two girls. 'Sounds a reasonable excuse for being a size 18' she thought as she wrote the information on the form. Then the questions became a little more personal. 'Mrs Grant, the next question is about body image. How do you feel about answering that?' There was a chuckle from the bed, followed by a grimace as Mrs Grant hastily held her stomach. 'I'd forgotten it hurt to laugh. Body image! Hmm. Have you time for a story?' Marie nodded and smiled encouragingly.

'If you'd asked me five years ago,' said Mrs Grant, 'I'd probably have simply said "yuk"! If you'd asked me four years ago, I'd have been too embarrassed to tell you why that changed. But now, well, I think I can tell you how it happened. One afternoon I was praying – my faith is really important to me. I wasn't aware of any needs of my own, and was probably saying a few prayers for a missionary friend. Suddenly, I found I was paralysed and helpless in a hospital bed. Not in pain, just scared. A man with a white tunic and longish hair appeared at the cubicle door. He had a very beautiful face, and I knew it was Jesus. I was delighted to have him as a visitor and expected him to come and sit down and have a chat. That would have been a real honour. Maybe he would cure me of whatever was wrong. But he stayed in the doorway smiling gently. Then I noticed he had a bowl of water and a towel. "I've come to give you your wash," he said. "Is that okay with you?" I was absolutely horrified by the idea, one of the male nurses, maybe, but Jesus!!! Out of the question! But on the other hand he had come to serve me – how could I say no to what he was offering? But on the other hand, how could I say yes? How totally embarrassing! He waited calmly, with a hint of amusement in his eyes as I struggled to find an answer to his question. Saying no would be saying no to his love, so eventually I managed to whisper a feeble "Yes, it's okay."

'He came to the bed and stood beside me. "I'm glad you can let me do this," he said. "I want to wash you with my love, to let you know how precious you are." He took my flannel from the rail on the back of my locker, found the soap from my sponge bag, and with the utmost gentleness began to wash me. I was still pretty uptight, but tried to relax – he was utterly comfortable with me. And as he washed my face and hands and arms the warmth of his presence and his love and the water all seemed to be inseparable. So far, so good. Then as he washed my feet and legs and body, I became aware that he was telling me quietly how beautiful I am, how each part of me has been designed by his Father, and how they both love me just exactly the way I am. That all sounded pretty far-fetched and I was unconvinced, but his touch and voice were healing something deep inside me. He dried me and smoothed in the talcum powder, combed my hair, fluffed up the pillow, and with a smile of pleasure and satisfaction turned to go.

'Suddenly, I was back in my own room and able to move. Stunned, shocked, I remembered what had happened. "And St Peter had problems with Jesus washing just his feet! How come he got let off so lightly!" I thought. "Dear God, nobody told me you do things like that! If you really want me to see myself as you see me, I've a lot of changing to do! Jesus was giving me so much love and appreciation. He wouldn't lie to me – and he said I'm beautiful! Help me believe it, help me see it ..." And I did make friends with my body, and let go the bad feelings about it that I'd had for as long as I could remember. I suppose it was a miracle in the end.'

They had finished the interview. The rest of the questions were fairly straightforward. 'Might have a sleep now,' said Mrs Grant. 'Maybe you don't believe stories like that, but it did happen. Now I'm really in hospital, and come to think of it, you girls were doing the same job this morning that Jesus did, and you were gentle too. Thank you for that, and for listening.' Her eyes closed. Marie touched her hand and said 'Thank you, I do believe your story, and I think it has something to do with me as well.'

And as the late afternoon sun shone on her shoulders Marie smiled at herself in the mirror. She threw her arms wide, then clasped herself in an embrace. 'You are beautiful' she told herself; 'God made you too, and what God has made is very good.'

June

Toitoi sparse like an old man's hair
Leaves in multiform death throes
Clawed brown hands beseeching skywards
Red rags and tatters hanging limp
Abundant gold cascading richly
On old grey graves
Silver trunk black tracery
And yes in there green sheen of belling tūī
Despite the starkness of dormancy
Skeletons have structural beauty
Hidden in summer
So have we in winters
When facades and fancy dress
Are ripped or wafted away
Leaving us naked and visible
Yet in all this
Chestnut buds are sticky with life
Sycamores a surprising pink
And inside grey fur magnolias
Get ready to dance.

My love for the
natural world
is a constant
inspiration and
source of hope.

Sharing the Journey – Growing in God through Spiritual Direction

A publicity article for the recently-formed Association of Christian Spiritual Directors, which I had joined. I love the times spent with people as they reflect on their soul-journeys.

Some time ago I was sensing a change in my prayer – the old way didn't seem to be 'working' any more. There seemed to be a bewildering array of other ways to 'do it,' and of books on 'how to.' I talked to my spiritual director about the confusion I was feeling. 'Have you talked to Jesus about this, and told him how you feel?' she asked.

I hadn't, of course, but went away to do so, not sure what, if anything, this would accomplish. 'Jesus' I said, feeling slightly foolish, 'I'm pretty confused about how to pray right now. It's like standing at a crossroad with a dozen roads all sign-posted to God. I don't have a clue which one to take.' Suddenly I had a sense of Jesus standing beside me at the crossroad saying, 'Hold my hand and close your eyes, and I will take you the way that's right for you.' I was awed by the new understanding that I was involved in a unique relationship, that there was a call to go on in trust that I would be guided, that all would be well.

What sort of relationship does God want to have with you? We are all different, so the quality of God's communication with each of us will be different also. Any important relationship in our lives deserves and benefits from time spent in reflection on its state, and on communication about each other's feelings and perceptions. A shining example of this principle is Marriage Encounter. On these weekends, partners spend time looking at themselves, each other, and the state of their relationship, and are given skills to continue with regular, honest communication.

Spiritual direction applies these same principles to an individual's relationship with God: as we reflect on it and acknowledge our feelings about it, God's communication with us is brought to our awareness. To reflect aloud on this with someone encourages further growth. Jesus' wish for us is that we receive life to the full. To quote Kenneth Leech, a modern writer on spiritual direction: 'It is the whole person who breathes, experiences, fears and worships God …. Psychological health is a necessary side-effect of religion, for salvation presupposes the health of the soul …. The aim of spiritual direction is the achievement of wholeness of life and integrated personality in which the inner and outer (persons) are united.' Our inner prayer-lives and our ordinary daily existence are intimately connected.

The idea of having guidance and support from another while discerning God's voice is richly endorsed in Scripture. Moses accepted advice from Jethro, his father-in-law, to appoint judges so that he could save his own energy for the representing of the People before God. And as a boy, the prophet Samuel lived in the Temple, under the care of Eli the priest. Three times in the night Yahweh called the boy's name, and each time

Samuel went to Eli thinking it was the old man who had called him, 'for he had as yet no knowledge of Yahweh.' Then Eli understood that it was the voice of God that Samuel was hearing, and instructed the boy to reply, 'Speak, Lord, your servant is listening.' And Yahweh spoke. In the gospels we see John the Baptist pointing people towards Jesus. Jesus acts in this role in many incidents – the Samaritan woman, Nicodemus, the rich young man, and his whole relationship with Peter. Another story rich with significance for spiritual direction is that of the raising of Lazarus from the dead. Jesus listens deeply to Martha and Mary. He prays and trusts that God at the right time will work a miracle. He calls on others to roll away the stone and later to unwrap the winding sheet – Lazarus' new life is to be revealed in the context of his everyday community. The 'Lazarus' in each one of us is called to new life – what is sick or dead in our humanity and spirit stirs, gets up, comes into the daylight to be unwrapped and loved into fullness to the glory of God.

Paul frequently urges Christians to encourage each other, to pray for and with each other. Later the Desert Fathers and monks and nuns were available to guide those who wished to know the ways of God. This ministry has always been an integral part of the church. However, for the last few hundred years, receiving spiritual direction has generally been seen as something that only priests and nuns do (or perhaps the occasional lay person who was heading for canonisation anyway!). 'Renew'[16] marked something of a change, when thousands of Catholics, traditionally reticent about discussing their own religious experiences, shared with each other how God is real for them. There has been further change in recent years – many ordinary folk, who are simply serious about God, have been finding spiritual direction a valuable way to enrich their prayer-lives. So the ministry of spiritual direction is once again filling its role at the heart of the church's mission – that of enabling each person to recognise and be intimate with his or her God.

The term 'direction' is actually a misnomer in the ordinary sense of the word. The very thing a spiritual director does not do is be directive. The director is there, in the beautiful Gaelic term, as a 'soul-friend,' a companion on the journey, and as someone who in an accepting, supportive way encourages the directee in relating to God in the way that is right for them. The director will help the directee to pay attention to God's personal communication with him or her, to respond to and grow in intimacy with this personally communicating God, and to live out the consequences of the relationship. A director will also pray for the directee, and be very clear that the primary role of guiding and supporting the seeker belongs to the Holy Spirit. Many of the thorny questions in our lives in the 1990s have to be worked out as we go along: What does God want me to do about this particular situation? How does God want me to pray? I've a sense there's more to God than I have known so far – how can I discover what else there is? Often there are no easy answers.

Being serious about God means giving these sorts of questions the serious attention they need, rather than popping them on the back burner for the umpteenth time. And this is where a spiritual director can help. A visit or two may be very useful, but the best value is gained from an ongoing, regular relationship with a director, so that together you can discern the call and movements of the Holy Spirit in the day-to-day rhythms of life as it unfolds. Finding a suitable soul-friend is made easier by the fact that there is now a National Association of Christian Spiritual Directors. It was founded in 1991 to encourage common standards in philosophy, ethics and values. Ongoing training and supervision are required for membership. Just over half the 80 or so present members are Catholics, with the rest being from a variety of denominations.

It is becoming more common for people who want a spiritual director to cross the denominational boundaries in a way that would have been unthinkable twenty years ago. When Father Gerard Hughes visits New Zealand later this year, this will be one of the main thrusts of his seminar. There is a profound unity between God-seekers, which can make the old divisions irrelevant. And the very nature of the relationship ensures that no moral, religious or spiritual values are imposed on the directee.

Another trend is for lay women and men to feel called to and be trained for this ministry, rather than limiting it exclusively to priests and religious as in the past. There are no theological barriers to this, and the lay experience can be very useful. The experience of being in spiritual direction is ideally one of feeling deeply heard and totally accepted. It is different in several important respects from counselling, and will not be a substitute where there is a major life problem to be worked out. The main focus is always the directee's relationship with God. As this is put into words and reflected on, the directee grows in sensitivity to the Voice within, and becomes more confident in saying, with Samuel, 'Speak, Lord, your servant is listening.'

Extrication!

The cobweb
Ethereal with diamond rainbows
Was nevertheless a death trap.
Attracted by its brilliance
I accepted the invitation to quench my thirst.
Danger-sense put aside
Mistaking it for solid ground
I flew right in
And the comforting warmth of being enfolded
Became in a leisurely measured way
A tomb.
Breaking the silence
With a last ditch call for help
Brought some relief
But that one too became enmeshed
Struggled and was still.
It's taken help much help and yet more help
To break away.
With understanding came new strength
And steel filament by steel filament
The breaking out the beginning to see
The spider host as black voracious
And not in the end
Omnipotent.
I have escaped!
The cobweb has been holed beyond repair
And I am cut and bruised and near to death
Antennae clogged and tangled
And wings too long bound down are crushed.
The unwinding the unbinding's underway
The extrication from the grubby tacky sticky
Bits of muck
Which still confine though losing power.
The possibility
Of the dream of the possibility of flying again
Becomes a dream.
For now simply to sit in the sun
Freed
Is enough.

Dealing with the tangled web created by the abusive counselling relationship and my complaint process seemed at last to be over. Regrettably it wasn't.

Women's Experience of Church Response to Family Violence – towards a theology for abusive marriages

Get up, said God, and take the child and his mother with you and escape into Egypt and stay there until I tell you, because Herod intends to search for the child and do away with him.

Matthew 2:13

Go, said God, get yourselves out of this life-threatening situation.

Last year was the Year of the Family, the year of 'Once were Warriors,' the year of Gay Oakes' conviction for murder. This year has already seen a number of women murdered by partners or ex-partners. Family violence is and has been in the news. It is very prevalent – the cases that hit the papers are the tip of a very large iceberg. It takes many forms – see the Power Wheel (Appendix 2) – and not all of them leave physical bruises. Emotional, economic and mental violence can also result in deep and crippling wounds. We have heard of the battered wife syndrome. There are Catholic women who have struggled with their consciences about whether or not to stay in abusive marriages, even if 'it's not that bad.' Or maybe they give up on church teaching they have heard as just not having any relevance to their situation. The political and social supports for male power are still part of the fabric of society and of the church.

I have counselled women who are or have been in violent relationships, and am co-facilitating a 10-week course for such women. This was developed in Duluth, Minnesota, as were the Power and Equality Wheels; and while there is a need in places to put it into New Zealand idiom, the principles and experiences are readily identified with by women here. There are three dimensions of abuse identified – the personal, the cultural and the institutional. Among the 'institutional supports for battering,' it concerns me to find the church mentioned along with the courts, the law and the police. This is obviously not aimed solely at the Catholic Church, but there are a number of Catholic women who have strongly related to the use of this phrase about their church. The police have been making substantial progress in changing their response to domestic violence, and there

While working as a facilitator with a Women's Learning Group, I was shocked to hear the church described as an 'institutional support for battering.' Exploring this concept gave me tools with which to understand the perspective of the women, and to understand better my own experience and attitudes. This paper was presented to Cardinal Williams in 1995 – I thought he would want to know what was being said and why. It was not until 2003 that the Bishops' Gender Issues Committee provided clergy in the Catholic Church with a significant education programme on domestic violence.

is an enquiry underway to pinpoint the difficulties women have with the legal system. I am suggesting that the Catholic Church should also listen carefully to women to discover how it is, despite its own goodwill, often experienced as contributing to their difficulties rather than helping them resolve their situations.

The kernel of the criticism is that the preached messages received from the church are part of what makes leaving a violent marriage more difficult than it already is. The questions 'why do they stay?' and 'why do they go back?' are often asked. It seems that the church must bear some responsibility in this area. What have they heard the church say about their situations? Or more importantly, what has it not been telling them in an open public way, to enable them to extricate themselves from situations that are at best demeaning, at worst life-threatening both emotionally and physically? There is information given in private pastoral situations which is not preached publicly, and this withholding of information is a form of collusion.

To assess this, and for my own interest, I have had a hard look at what really happens and what gets said and, more importantly, what does not get said. I have looked at the current social situation, resources presently available to Catholics with violent marriages, Catholic teaching on marriage, Catholic literature on marriage difficulties, and an alternative set of gospel principles, which if publicly preached and taught, would enable women to recognise their choices with greater clarity. And enable men to hear that abuse of power within families is not acceptable!

The truly helpful, healing response to a woman, whose personal power has been eroded almost out of existence by domestic violence, is to see that she knows she has choices and that she will be supported in the making of them. Has the teaching church hitherto done an adequate job of this? I believe not.

Publication of the Bishops' letter on domestic violence in *Welcom* (the Wellington Archdiocesan paper) in October 1992, and the accompanying article by the Director of Catholic Social Services was a huge step forward. The Director's article was a wonderfully pertinent description of the situation. She had a concern about church response and said that clients had been unable to find support or protection within their church community. The members of this community also need to hear a public teaching on family violence; much pain can be inflicted on those already under severe stress by well-meaning, idealistic Catholics who think – and sometimes say – 'it's best if she goes back.'

In the Bishops' letter, much genuine concern was expressed and appropriate advice given to potential pastoral listeners. The assurance that 'it can be a faithful and loving action to take positive steps to end the violence of the situation' is a welcome move towards encouraging a positive, self-preserving path for women. But firstly it stops short of presenting leaving as a Godly choice, and secondly puts the responsibility for ending the violence onto the woman. The impression I have from talking to a number of priests is that while they are happy to explore the option of leaving a violent marriage in a private pastoral setting, they feel any public statements of that nature would be tantamount to encouraging marriage break-down. 'It would cause all sorts of problems,' said one. Who for? I wonder.

I believe that not having an appropriate and publicly preached teaching on the rightness of doing whatever is necessary for self-preservation from violence, including leaving the marriage permanently, and only giving this information privately is a form of collusion with the violence. It is withholding information that could prove empowering by letting the woman know she has church-affirmed choices she may not otherwise realise. So the teaching church must publicly tell women in violent marriages that their cause is God's cause – not just by giving them permission to leave and forgiveness for their 'failure,' a demeaning 'God will let you off under the circumstances, dear.' It must be said loudly and clearly: 'Our God, our compassionate, liberator God wants you out of there, wants you to get out of a situation where your health, life and sanity are endangered, where your children's security is impossible, to a place where you can live in peace and dignity.' I believe God's justice requires the church to affirm positively the women who with almost their last gasp have summoned up the enormous courage to escape from continuing violence, to face an unknown future, which will undoubtedly involve poverty, traumatic dealings with the legal system and maybe the church Marriage Tribunal, and the sheer hard work of solo parenting.

For Catholics in violent marriages the main resources provided by the church are pastoral care within parishes, its social services agencies, Retrouvaille, the weekend retreat for people with troubled marriages, and if there is a divorce, the Marriage Tribunal.

The first two are undoubtedly useful in the majority of cases. I know that many women who approach a parish priest for help in these circumstances find support in the ways recommended in the Bishops' letter: being taken seriously, simplistic solutions avoided, etc. Catholic Social Services continues to do a fine job, as described in *Welcom* of May 1995. The Director states that 'there is an underlying feeling sometimes conveyed to the agency that it encourages women to be too independent, to leave their marriages and to break the laws of the church.' And that none of these things is true! I wonder whose accusations these are, and what church teaching they have heard.

Retrouvaille insists that the available problem-specific treatment programmes are undertaken for violence, and drug and alcohol abuse by intending participants where applicable, as a condition of their being accepted for the weekend.

When a marriage has finally broken down, there is the option of applying for an annulment, once the legal divorce is through. I have found considerable resistance among women to approaching the Marriage Tribunal. There are a number of reasons for this: Cost. It is not generally known that the cost is negotiable to some degree. If a woman is living with children on the Domestic Purposes Benefit, simple financial survival is usually what life is about.

Resistance to the idea, officially inaccurate but nonetheless widespread, that by declaring the marriage null the children thereby become deemed as illegitimate.

Some women feel 'too honest' to apply for an annulment – they are convinced in their own minds that a marriage had in fact existed initially.

To go through this in-depth procedure is traumatic in itself. To opt into it two or more years after the separation puts at risk whatever emotional security and calm has been developed in that time. Some public-relations work on behalf of the Tribunal could correct popular misconceptions.

So there is considerable provision of support services once the situation has arisen. But what is taught or not taught that permits or encourages the situations to develop in the first place?

The teaching of the church on marriage is unequivocal: it is indissoluble – until death do us part. It is, in the traditional words, for better, for worse, for richer, for poorer, in sickness and in health. In other words difficulties are normal, to be expected and not ever to be used as an 'out'. God's part in the sacrament of matrimony is described as giving all the grace necessary to cope with whatever happens within the marriage.

Forgiveness, and repeated forgiveness, is the inferred desirable response to transgressions, be they adultery, alcoholism, verbal, emotional or economic abuse or physical violence. Received guidelines for married relationships include such concepts as: unconditional and self-sacrificial love, carrying one's cross, giving is to be 100 percent, commitment no matter what, turning the other cheek, washing feet, the wife being subject to her husband (even if this is now usually described as part of mutual submission) – the only adequate reason to deny a spouse marital rights, according to St Paul, being 'for prayer.' Other quotes are 'never let the sun go down on your anger' (kiss and make up), 'love is saying yes,' 'any two parents are better than one,' 'God is into healing marriages,' 'prayer works miracles,' and 'you've made your bed, you lie in it.'

This sort of teaching is what is described as 'institutional supports for battering.' There must obviously be teaching of ideals, but ideals can become idols to be preserved at all costs, and in many marriages these costs have been to the women and children. Such scriptural models for a violent marriage relationship as the flight into Egypt, the Exodus, and Jesus' anger towards the Pharisees and traders in the Temple would be considerably more useful!

A look back at some marriage literature proved both interesting and shocking.

1. In *The Catholic Marriage Manual* (Kelly, 1962), the recommended handbook when I married, some permissions are given so grudgingly that they are abusive in themselves:

    > In an extreme case the wife (of an alcoholic) may find it necessary to leave him to protect herself and the children. She should not take this drastic step without first consulting her spiritual adviser, because leaving an alcoholic to his own feeble resources often causes him to drink even more and makes recovery all but impossible. (pp135-6).

    > Even when an innocent victim has a legal right to live apart from an erring spouse it is often unwise to do so. This may be especially true when a partner has expressed sorrow for his adultery and promises not to repeat it. Although a wife may legally separate, by doing so she may deny her children the advantage of their father's companionship. Her refusal to engage in bodily communion with her husband may lead to future sins of adultery by him and

possibly even by herself. By insisting upon the right to live apart, she may show a lack of the Christian virtue of forgiveness. (p157)

> If separation is counselled … it should never be presumed to be for life. Our faith teaches that there is always hope for the greatest sinners: adulterers repent and drunkards reform and sometimes they become even more virtuous than they have ever been. The possibility of reconciliation should never be ruled out. If God willingly forgives the repentant sinner, one of his creatures should not refuse to do so. (p158)

The burden of taking responsibility for the man's welfare is given to the woman with no regard to the cost to her. As Women's Refuge workers know only too well, repentance is an integral part of the cycle of violence. So is inappropriate forgiveness!

2. Twenty years later in 1981, Jack Dominian in *Marriage, Faith and Love* has come to grips with the problem of abusive marriages with a bit more realism. He states that a spouse may have to leave the matrimonial home to show their spouse they mean business where there is gambling, excessive drinking, lack of affection or serious affronts to dignity. This is recommended sooner rather than later. But he still goes on to state:

> If the husband drifts downwards through mental illness, alcoholism or crime, his work suffers and the standards of the whole family fall. The spouse may leave and label the partner as 'no good.' The vow to stay with one's spouse for better or worse applies particularly in these circumstances. A husband needs the support of his wife to escape a bad patch. (p206)

Neither controlling behaviour nor violence is even mentioned in his index.

3. In the same year, 1981, comes another mixed message from Donald Nicholl in his book, *Holiness*. In a discussion on responsibility he rightly questions the scenario where 'the suffering partner so very often appeared to be noble and to be putting up with the other partner's bad behaviour quite heroically.' And states: 'no human being should allow himself [sic] to be treated like that … you should never allow your humanity to be insulted in that way. In all our actions there is both a personal and representative element.' But later he writes: 'when suffering appears on our horizon it is a sign that we are considered worthy to serve as sacrificial lambs, pure so that we can penetrate into the lives of others without harming them, even into the most evil places.' (p152) A call to martyrdom in the cause of sanctity!

4. Recent teaching on marriage breakdown in New Zealand includes the Bishops' letter 'When Dreams Die' (1987), which was reprinted in the *Marist Messenger* in April 1993. An apparently clear statement: 'The church's teaching on the indissolubility and fidelity of marriage needs to be seen alongside her teaching on the need for compassion and understanding towards those in any kind of difficulty.' It is difficult to avoid the message: 'we will offer our compassion and support, but from the position of regretting your decision, should you decide to separate.'

5. The same message is inherent in Pope John Paul II's document, 'The Christian Marriage in the Modern World' (1981), which states clearly: 'This union as well as the good of the children imposes total fidelity on both spouses and argues for the unbreakable oneness.' He talks of the effects of divorce being guilt, grief and loneliness, and states that the church will minister to the individual's grief and anger until they find the courage to forgive. These people may then find their own vocation in ministering to fellow parishioners who are 'victims of marriage breakdown.' While there are undoubtedly many situations where both parties could be said to be victims of the marriage breakdown, I want to focus on those situations where a woman, and usually children as well, are victims not of a situation but of a violent husband and father. The effects of divorce for them, far from guilt can be a measure of security, safety, relief and some sort of hope for normality. The response from the church, which would help them heal, is a simple public affirmation of the courage and the Godly appropriateness of leaving a violent marriage.

The most helpful alternative framework I have been able to find for these situations is that of The Kairos Document (1985), which is a theological reflection on the then political crisis in South Africa. I see this as applicable to the lack of public church teaching on violent marriages. It contrasts the Christian 'stock ideas' of reconciliation and peace, justice and non-violence ('church theology'), with the need for a 'prophetic theology,' which describes as sin any attempt 'to persuade those of us who are oppressed to accept our oppression and become reconciled to the intolerable crimes committed against us.' And 'like Jesus we must expose this false peace.' As his disciples 'we should rather promote truth and justice and life at all costs, even at the cost of creating conflict, disunity and dissension along the way … .' Marriages may break up as a result! No forgiveness is possible without repentance. If the oppressor does ever introduce reforms that might lead to real change, this will come about because of strong pressure from those who are oppressed.

True justice, God's justice, demands a radical change of structures. This can only come from below, from the oppressed themselves. Oppression is described as the experience of being 'crushed, degraded, humiliated, exploited, impoverished, defrauded, deceived and enslaved.' Strong words, which we can readily recognise as being the experience of South African blacks. How easily do we recognise them as describing our next-door neighbour or even perhaps that of a family member? 'It cannot be taken for granted that everyone who is oppressed has taken up their own cause and is struggling for their own liberation.' 'Nor,' says The Kairos Document, 'can it be assumed that all oppressed Christians are fully aware of the fact that their cause is God's cause.' '[The church] must then help people to understand their rights and their duties. There must be no misunderstanding about the moral duty of all who are oppressed to resist oppression and to struggle for liberation and justice.'

My question is what can the teaching church do to make sure women (and men) in violent relationships are aware of all this? When is the church going to repent of its perhaps unwitting collusion with male violence within marriage, recognise that many of its respected members lead double lives, and call them to take responsibility for their actions and seek appropriate re-education? Will it speak prophetically to their wives and children – not just 'You don't have to put up with that,' but 'Wake up! There is a road to freedom. You may choose to pack your bag, take your kids and go. God wants you safe. You do not have to stay and endure death in any of its forms.'

Quotes to Ponder

But when the traumatic events are of human design those who bear witness are caught in the conflict between victim and perpetrator. It is morally impossible to remain neutral in this conflict. The by-stander is forced to take sides. It is very tempting to take the side of the perpetrator. All the perpetrator asks is that the bystander do nothing. He appeals to the universal desire to see, hear and speak no evil. The victim on the contrary asks the bystander to share the burden of pain. The victim demands action, engagement, remembering. (Hermans, 1992. p7)

The kenosis model of servanthood, self-emptying and humbling (Philippians 2:6-7) is perhaps viable for (middle-class) men, but further victimises women. This is a popular model with liberal men, even liberationists. It may allow them to enter the oppressed state of the other, as servant and in service. Women, however, are already other, humbled, humiliated, and sanctifying this only reiterates their lower and forever lowly status. (Dale, 1994. p43)

Recommendations

- That teaching/preaching be scrutinised for anything that encourages women to see staying in a violent relationship as somehow 'more Catholic' than leaving.

- That there be positive preaching on the necessity for challenging oppression as it exists in homes, with personal safety as a prime consideration.

- That priests explore their own attitudes to male/female roles, either as participants in the normal Men for Non-violence courses, or by a course run by Men for Non-violence facilitators.

- That by reading the mentioned books, and coming to understand what does in fact help women, they will give those principles priority over attempting to preserve marriages.

Recommended Reading

Douglas, Kay (1994) *Invisible Wounds – a self-help guide for New Zealand women in destructive relationships*. Penguin, Auckland

Hermans, Judith Lewis (1992) *Trauma and Recovery*. Basic Books

The Kairos Theologians (1985) *The Kairos Document: Challenge to the Church*. Catholic Institute for International Relations. United Kingdom

Ambivalence

God, I'm confused!
They told me that if
I prayed and met you in the Eucharist
You'd come to lead and teach
And so you have
And then I'd see you
Feel you know you
In all I meet
And so it is
I would know you
In gull-sweep gales
The pounding surf
Each grain of sand
And so I do
Why now has it become so hard
To find you in a church?
You are too real
In each nook cranny atom and breath
To become any more real
In bread on Sundays
It's so hard to go from
Christ-in-flesh
To Christ-in-Bread
To a male God
Who is AlmightyKingLordJudge
We receive each other
You and I
Beside the beds of the dying
With abused women
As they learn they matter
In the counselling room
In the tears
And the moments of glory
In the miracle of hearts
And minds that open to
New compassion for self
And maybe others

This first
acknowledgement
of the possibility of
leaving my lifetime
church was written
during a precious few
months as chaplain at
Mary Potter Hospice.
It was in response to
the edict from Rome
that there would never
be women priests. My
question: what am I
condoning by staying
in the church?

Do I have to stay in the dry place?
Am I being dishonest in being there
And believing differently?
How can I stay
When priestly women are eliminated
Forever at the stroke of a pen?
But they say 'Don't go
We need you!'
Yet I begin to understand
As never before
All those who say
I've moved beyond the church
Or even beyond Christianity
I'm left with simply this:
A God who daily gets more
Awesome astonishing unconfined
And a human Jesus-Friend
Thereby all the more crucial!

Aftermath

That phase of the storm is over
I found my anger
And let it rip – civilly, in printed words
I found in the love of listeners
A lens that sparked my pain
What more can happen?
The saga must have run its course
I want to let it go soon, please, God
I want to learn to trust again
To be normal with no dark secrets
On my back and in my gut
And in my blood churning round and round
And in each brain cell like a magnet
Powering through iron filings
Pulling them into line
The one track mind with no let-up
Sticking them tight, so tight
They can't even be scraped off

Letting secrets see daylight
Is like lifting the stone off a nest of maggots
They squirm with frantic life
But soon starved of darkness
And filth and putrid rottenness
They'll wither and die
Leaving clean new growth
The scar tissue might need a miracle
But miracles happen
God of miracles
Find me someone to love

God, see to him:
The man I loved was never there
Only a paper facade of caring
A wolf masquerading as grandmother,
And Little Red Riding Hood
Too naive, trusting and polite
What big ears you've got, Grandmama!
To hear my pain and make me feel loved
But why the lecherous interest in my sexuality?
You're wise – you must know it's what I need!
What big eyes you've got, Grandmama!

The abuse had cast
a very long shadow
on my life, and the
struggles to deal
with its effects and
subsequent events not
instigated by me were
still not over.

They seem to shine with lust not love
No – that's impossible, you're God's anointed
I must be imagining things!
What big teeth you've got, Grandmama!
A smile to hearten me and make me relax
A prelude to being gobbled up, chewed, used
And spat out

See to him, God
See to his blindness
See to his hard heart
See to his thick skin
See to his conscience
See to his pain
See to his unawareness
See to his reputation
See to his misused power
See to his victims
See to his family
See to his parishioners
See to his church
See to the healings
God of truth, justice and compassion

'Takes two to tango'
Has no connection at all with what
happened
It was more like being a fish hooked
Struggling and reeled in
More like being a starving child
In a room with ice-cream, fruit and
chocolate cake
All laced with arsenic
Needing food even while
Recognising the smell and taste of death
More like being a rabbit
Mesmerised in headlights
By an oncoming car
Unable to escape
Trapped in a fenceless space
Questions of 'Why couldn't you...?
Why didn't you...?
Have no relevance or answers
Except the overwhelming power
Of power misused
There was no choice

To share the howl of outrage
With the others
Helps me howl
It dispels the loneliness
Of being scapegoated
By those who should have cared
And helped and healed –
Not added fuel to his fire
By accusing lying frightening
Bulldozing steam-rollering harrowing
Nailing gagging isolating
And casting into outer darkness
Hoping that truth
Could thus be smothered and disposed of
But truth is a phoenix
And will not be extinguished
It rises gains new life and strength
It turns on those who thought to kill it
And sings its story to the world!

Journey with AIDS

The participants in the Women's Support Group at the AIDS Foundation's Awhina Centre were asked to write the stories of their AIDS Journey. My experiences had moved me deeply – so many learnings, so many wonderful people!

In 1990, when I first discovered someone I knew had AIDS, there was a lot more fear around than exists now. I too was afraid. Because I was in a support role as an industrial chaplain, I knew I needed to be able to get involved, and to deal first with my fear and discomfort before doing so, both for my sake and for the sake of those with whom I would come into close contact. I was fortunate to have two wise women accessible. One had already accompanied a man with AIDS through to his death, and continued to support the partner, himself HIV positive. Her advice was 'to get in there and do some loving,' and that I'd 'be the one to gain.' The other, a nun whom I'd known for some years, was the Education Officer and Human Rights Advocate at the AIDS Foundation's Awhina Centre. She gave me written information, reassurance about safety, and lots of encouragement.

But that came later. My first task was to assure the man – I'll call him Mike – of my support and willingness to learn. He told me about his partner Jack, and I realised that to be truly there for Mike would mean loving Jack too. I had had no previous contact with a gay couple, and it was not the easiest transition in the world. There were a series of adjustments: one was when I visited their flat and the double bed made me confront an aspect of their life that I had not wanted to think about. Another was the realisation later that not only had I come to love them both, but that the quality of their relationship far surpassed that of a lot of heterosexual marriages. The caring, the communication, the forgiveness (as one, and I did not know which, had infected the other with the virus). How many marriages, I wondered, could survive a crisis of that magnitude? I was also overwhelmed by the acceptance and unity in Mike's family. His nieces and nephews simply had two uncles in that household, his mother referred to Jack as her son-in-law. I felt a great deal of admiration for them all.

It was some months before a question surfaced for me: what if it were one of my four sons? How could I ever cope? Having known Mike's family, I realised I would have some idea where to start. It would be devastatingly sad, but it would not be the end of the world. We would not be alone – there would be an astonishing network of love and practical support available. It had the potential to bring out the best in the family.

From time to time I was still afraid. I knew in my head that catching the virus by normal social contact was impossible. But medical science had been known to make mistakes before – what if they were wrong about this? I had to make leaps into faith on a number of occasions, the most memorable of which was sharing a home communion service with a friend who had AIDS and his minister. A special bond grew out of that occasion – we all had a deep sense of God-with-us.

Then came my first experience of a Candlelight Memorial. It was on Pentecost Sunday, 1991, and it blew my mind! This is the traditional Christian feast to remember the coming of the Holy Spirit in tongues of flame to Christ's fearful disciples. This experience empowered them to be able to go out to teach and preach and transcend normal social barriers. I recognised the same dynamic and images at work that evening with the ring of huge torch flames on the forecourt at Parliament. There was no sleep that night – it was like being in labour, and what came to birth was a poem.

Candlelight Memorial

There is darkness here, the darkness of dis-ease
A shadowed huddle of strangers not yet one
We light our lamps while wondering at the calm
And flickering faces become friends
And may-be-friends
The dark recedes
There is a woman
Who speaks with authority
From having worked and served and loved
Who proclaims my God
As Love, as Cure, for Love drives out the fear
Men speak of walls of language, race, sex, age and class
Being broken down by love and guts
In the face of common pain
Then the fire comes
As we remember the dead to the tolling of the bell
The fire comes
Each one carrying a Calvary cross
For someone dear
The fire comes
Bringing light of Easter victory
The fire comes – and still it comes –
Torch-bearers for those gone, a race still being run
The fire comes
To a song of peace – Dona nobis pacem
And in our midst a ring of flames

Flames of strength and faith and love
Separate flames but of one Fire
Celebrate with sparkling stars
Celebrate fear gone and darkness drowned
Celebrate life and hope with power
Celebrate with flying stars
Pentecost now!

The following Sunday, despite my intense dislike of public speaking, I felt compelled to stand up at my local church and describe my Pentecost conversion experience: I had experienced the God who prefers to be with marginal people as being powerfully present in Parliament grounds that night. I appealed to the compassion and common sense of the people I knew, and prepared them a little for the day when they would discover that a neighbour, friend, workmate or family member would be living with the virus. When I finished there was applause.

Later that year Jack died, and a few weeks later so did Mike. Jack's mother came to be with her son and once again I was over-awed by the strength and compassion of the two mothers – for each other and for both their sons. About that time on retreat I saw a section of the video of 'Jesus of Nazareth.' It stopped with a frame of Mary holding the dead body of her son. Again, the images started whirring away inside. Jesus too died in his early thirties like Mike and Jack; like them he experienced exclusion by and from the establishment; and no doubt like their mothers, Mary had to struggle too, not understanding, sharing the exclusion, but loving anyway. 'He's my son, he's a good person, and nothing changes that.' And so 'Good Friday' came to be written.

Good Friday

> Son, I conceived you in joy – but not for this.
> For nine months bore you – but not for this.
> Laboured and gave you birth – but not for this.
> Fed you, washed you, dressed you – but not for this.
> Played with you, laughed with you – but not for this.
> Encouraged you, kissed you better – but not for this.
> Planned for you, dreamed for you – but not for this.
>
> There was to be strength, long years, a purpose,
> Sons of your own in time.
> Care perhaps for me when old.
> Times of peace and pain, of loss, of gain – not this.
>
> But somewhere in this crazy screaming grief
> A still point of tiny light exists
> As I begin somehow to see
> Inevitability of who you most deeply were
> Called you to this time.
> You could not do otherwise
> Than be true to yourself, my son.
> I understand.
> It was for this.

Something I realised at the time of Jack's death was the total lack of community sanction and support for the grieving survivor of a homosexual relationship. Where there has been a committed relationship, what is experienced by the survivor is nothing more or less than widowhood, with all the pain that this entails. This is not infrequently complicated by legal wrangles over wills, and tension with the partner's family. When my husband died there was a great out-pouring of love and support. I couldn't imagine going through that experience in isolation.

Meeting the other members of Mike and Jack's peer support group was enriching. I was shy at first, only knowing them as men living with the virus, but not wanting to simply identify them like that. Gradually I came to appreciate them as talented, caring, courageous people whose lives had acquired a quality rarely seen in the world where life is assumed to be unlimited.

I had been brought up with a traditional Catholic view, 'You as a homosexual are acceptable, any homosexual activity is not.' But as I looked and listened and pondered, I came to something more like 'God in infinite wisdom creates many people homosexual, so how can sexual expression be denied them?' I became convinced traditional Christian theology did not match the reality of the lived experience of these men, my friends with AIDS. 'Sin' presupposes choice. But they said their gayness 'just is' – no choice in the matter. As I 'did theology,' as my 'faith sought understanding,' I was impressed by David Bromell's plea (Love Unbounded, pp26-30) for established principles of Christian social justice teaching to be applied to gays and lesbians. He goes on to say: 'Participation is the key to a just resolution of Christian ethical reflection on homosexuality. Any church that makes decisions about us without allowing us to participate fully and equally in that process of decision making has decided unjustly, and its morality is immoral.'

The development of this process is making somewhat slow progress in the Christian churches of Aotearoa New Zealand. When I put together the prayers of intercession for Mike's funeral service, I brought one that read: 'We pray that the church open its heart and mind to the gay community with respect and acceptance.' This didn't seem particularly radical to me, but the officiating minister forbade me to use it. I was torn about whether to accept this ruling, but decided it was in the interests of the family not to have the minister, already nervous about having a church full of gays, agitated further. He had been a good supportive friend to the guys and to their mothers, and went on to give support to others in the group as well, but a public prayer of acceptance was deemed 'too political.'

Advocacy work at grass roots level within the church can be very rewarding. I was invited to help run a workshop on AIDS for the Catholic Women's League. I, in my ignorance, had thought of them as the cake-icing brigade. I couldn't have been more wrong. As preparation for the workshop we had asked them to ponder the scenario where their son came back from overseas and said 'Mum, I'm gay. This is my partner. And we're both HIV positive.' Then the questions: what would you be feeling? What would you be thinking? What would you need? They had done their homework, and when with permission I told them Mike and Jack's story there were tears as they recognised that this had been real life for many a family. They went away less afraid and more in touch with their own compassion and priorities. They were magnificent! And recently in a parish that prides itself on being open minded, as part of an adult education series I'd helped plan, a gay man came to speak on his experience of being gay and Catholic. Change inches along!

The Women's Support Group at the Awhina Centre came into being, and again my life has been enriched by the courage and compassion of women whose lives have been more closely affected by the virus than mine. I am there as a friend of the men I've known who have died, as a supporter (and admirer) of the wives, mothers, daughters and HIV positive women, and as a counsellor. Someone suggested, 'Maybe you could write a poem about the group.' And at 3 o'clock the next morning I woke up and 'Cairn' came about. The title and image came from the piles of stones that mark a path or stand as a memorial.

I feel privileged to have been on the edges of the HIV/AIDS community and to have seen the sort of love that is possible in the face of a common enemy. It is hard to explain to people in the 'ordinary world,' which is built on the ideals of self-sufficiency, success and immortality, what there could be of value in being with people who are learning to live with the virus and know their life expectancy is now curtailed. Despite diseases that range from the irritating to the truly horrific, most work towards a quality of life that is truly amazing. Love, courage and inspiration abound.

I did 'get in there and do some loving,' and I have received infinitely more than I have given, and have indeed been the one to gain!

Cairn

Here is a cairn
Of women
Who've climbed still climb
And climb again
Not from choice
The craggy mountain
Carrying stones
Hard stones
Jagged stones
Impossible stones
With each other
To the top
Wounded weary teary
Wracked by sunsets
Yet glimpsing now and then
The mystery
Of a wider view
The cairn grows
The cairn glows now
Lit from within
With what each brings
And becomes beacon of hope
For travellers
Struggling in the dark

Whatsoever You Do... A tribute to AIDS Campaigner Tom O'Donoghue

As an industrial chaplain I met a young man who had AIDS, and then became involved with the HIV/AIDS community. In the early 1990s there was still huge fear. I learned much about love and marginalisation and the choice of the gospel Jesus during this association. It was a privilege!

God is Love. God is Aroha. And that being so, God was present in Tom O'Donoghue's dealings with people during his life, and tangibly present at his funeral in Old St Paul's, Wellington, on 1 October 1994. His death as a result of AIDS received national attention on television and radio and in the newspapers. He had been committed to HIV/ AIDS education for the previous six years, since his own diagnosis with HIV. He was a crusader in the campaign to prevent the spread of HIV/AIDS, and to make life more bearable and whole for those who have contracted the virus.

I did not know him well, but his courage in speaking out at the Candlelight Memorials had made a deep impression on me. He was the first person I heard say publicly, 'I am a gay man and I am HIV positive.' That was on Pentecost Sunday in 1991, in Parliament grounds, and the ring of flaming torches that night reminded me of the tongues of fire at the first Pentecost. I had the sense that the Spirit of Love was again conquering fear, breaking down barriers, creating a community of acceptance and respect in the face of ostracism and fear from various sections of our society.

Tom spoke again at the Candlelight Memorials in 1992, and in 1993, when he said, 'I now have AIDS.' In 1994, once again Pentecost Sunday, he was still there, despite being very ill. This time his message was one of encouragement to HIV positive people to disclose their status. While doing this would obviously be very stressful with the still-prevalent prejudices, he urged people to take this risk as being a healthier path than living with the burden of keeping the secret, as well as that of the virus itself. He died that September.

As people spoke about Tom at his funeral, his impact on people – all sorts of people – emerged from the stories we heard. A young man who has AIDS told how Tom had changed his life by encouraging disclosure. 'Because of that,' he said, 'I was able to find the courage to go and tell my mum. It was okay. She is supporting me now. I wish I had done it five years ago.'

Alexis, a member of the transgender community said: 'Tom saved my life. He stopped me from committing suicide. He taught me to look inside myself and throw away some rubbish and value the rest.' She went on, 'Look at the people beside you and around you: when we see each other, when we see each other in town, let's say Hi!'

Katherine O'Regan, the then Associate Minister of Health, told of the many times Tom had been in her office, lobbying, persuading, being an advocate for the rights of people living with HIV/AIDS, for prisoners, prostitutes, drug users, transvestites and transexuals. She cried. This had obviously been more than a bureaucratic exchange – she had felt the impact of his humanity, knowledge and crusading spirit.

A speaker from the Justice Department, responsible for the AIDS education and prevention programme in prisons, spoke of how Tom had taught her how to respect and relate to people belonging to marginalised minorities.

There were the lighter moments too. A friend from way back described Tom as a man who enjoyed a good time, a party vulture. Then added, peering at the bronze bird of the lectern, 'Speaking of vultures …'

Catherine from the Prostitutes Collective remembered Tom's gift for bringing together groups who had had little or no contact with each other to a place of mutual respect and cooperation.

Fellow workers from the People Living with AIDS Union, of which he was a founding member, committed themselves to carrying on his work, to keeping his memory alive as a Beacon of Hope for those left here, and for those still to come.

So there we were, gays, lesbians and straight, public servants, prostitutes, transgender people, intravenous drug users, people living with HIV and AIDS, nuns, ex-prisoners, family, co-workers, friends, all united in our love and respect for this remarkable man. Tom was not religious, someone said, but he was deeply spiritual, with a particular affinity recently for the Buddhist way. While respecting his understanding of his own journey, I need to express my understanding of Tom's life and work in my Christian language:

> I was hungry and you gave me food; I was thirsty and you gave me drink; I was a stranger and you made me welcome, naked and you clothed me, sick and you visited me, in prison and you visited me.
>
> *(Matthew 25:35-40)*

And

> He has sent me to bring the good news to the poor, to proclaim liberty to captives and to the blind new sight, to set the downtrodden free.
>
> *(Luke 4:18)*

Tom lived and worked among some of the most stigmatised and marginalised people in our society. He fed them with love and hope; quenched their thirst with his compassion; when they felt isolated and marginalised by the virus he drew them into the community of care and mutual support he had been instrumental in forming; he clothed them and taught them to clothe themselves and each other with the garment of respect. He was an empowerer, an enabler who opened people's eyes to their own human value by the way he interacted with them. He showed them how to live honestly, courageously and freer from fear, and fought for their rights as human beings. They called him Teacher and Rangatira.

This was a Christ-like life, if ever there was one! Again at the funeral I had the same sense of the Spirit of God at work in and through Tom, breaking down divisions, enabling all present to discover at greater depth their own capacity for love, respect, courage and the forming of community. Another Pentecost experience!

Tom O'Donoghue packed so much into that six years from his HIV positive diagnosis until his death. Since then he has been missed and remembered. His spirit and example will continue to enrich and inspire all those who know that their time on this planet is limited by the virus. He has also given me, and undoubtedly others, cause to ponder about Pharisees and tax-collectors, about labels and judgements and condemnations, and about where the Jesus of the gospels is truly to be found …

Reproach

God, I've a bone to pick with you!
I can see that after all this pain (mine and others')
Your church is going to be a better place.
I know that in my youthful fervour
I said 'use me'
So I can't blame you for taking me at my word,
But that's not the point.
Right now it seems that you are just one more
Of the array of abusive men
The world is riddled with.
Why did you make them like that –
Lust-driven and blind?
Made in your image – are you like that too?
How come when I put myself trustingly into your hands
I ended up in his?
Okay, I've learnt a lot
But that's not the point
I've learnt a lot about respect
About consultation, permission and
boundaries.
Right now I feel you manipulated me
Into a too tough place.
How come you didn't consult me
About whether I wanted to be a leading
player
In a nine-year nightmare?
I was consulting you at every step of the way
And still it happened.
I can now smell power, discrimination,
unawareness
From a hundred kilometres.
Which is why I'm taking a break
From your church's Sunday doings
Where you are almost invariably a man.
Not a break from you – that's impossible.
But I do need you
To redeem yourself in my eyes
Show me how to trust you again
How to live without fear of what you might
do next.

Once my anger about the abuse finally arrived, God came in for His share. I could not simply walk away from the relationship with Him, however tempting the idea!

I need healing
But looking to others for healing
Is to risk more hurt
That's how it all happened
in the first place.
So there is a wall of scar tissue
That needs to be dissolved.
You have my permission to see to it
But please be very gentle! And respectful!

First Australasian Conference on Sexual Abuse by Health Professionals and Members of the Clergy

In Sydney in April, 300-400 people gathered to share their learning and experience on the subject of sexual abuse by members of the clergy and health professionals. Organisational incest, one speaker called it. That there could be an international conference of this sort is a significant step in the readiness of both church and secular agencies to acknowledge and address this issue. Progress is being made in developing the justice-making process after damaging breaches of trust and professional responsibility by ministers, church workers and professionals.

In 1995 I was invited to join the Catholic Complaints Committee (then known as the Protocol Committee) as the survivor representative, and attended the Sydney Conference on sexual abuse described below. I brought back much useful information and valuable contacts, both for the church and for my own ongoing healing, and wrote this article for the Wellington Archdiocesan paper, *Welcom*. My hopes of progress have taken a long time and intensive media pressure to bear much fruit.

The international line-up included experts in analysis and treatment, such as Marie Fortune, Gary Schoener and Ellen Luepker from USA, a church delegation from Norway, and a member of a survivor group from England as a special representative of Cardinal Hume. Mainstream churches were represented, as were lawyers, counsellors, doctors and mental-health professionals, and at the centre of concern were the survivors. They were both male and female; the men who spoke had been abused as children, and the women had been abused as children or as adults.

Three members of the Auckland Survivors' Advocacy Support Group presented a very moving workshop, 'Survivors – the Prophetic Voice.' This prophetic role was acknowledged many times by the professionals present, as the struggle to redress past abuse and create safer church communities is being engaged with increasing energy. Another Auckland grouping presented a model of an education workshop to raise awareness of the issues, using Marie Fortune's video 'Not in my Church.' It is the survivors who have the courage to lay a complaint about what has happened to them who are enabling the churches to investigate allegations, discipline perpetrators, offer healing, and engage in prevention and education.

Also interesting were presentations on Australian Catholic experience. Dr Neil Ormerod, lay theologian and co-author (with his partner Thea) of the book, *When Ministers Sin – Sexual Abuse in the Churches*, documented the evolving attitudes of the episcopal and diocesan response in New South Wales over the last eight years. Realisation by the hierarchy is growing that professional responsibility is at stake when dealing with complaints of sexual abuse. His paper was titled 'A little breathless and a little late.'

Mrs Helen Last, Coordinator of the Pastoral Response Team in the Melbourne Archdiocese presented the well-developed pastoral strategies in place there. A 17-page document describes the availability of 'Assistance in Response to Courage.' It details care (advocacy, emotional and spiritual) for the primary victims/survivors, for the secondary victims, for example, parents, spouse, etc of the victim, also for the members of a parish where there has been sexual abuse by a minister.

Marie Fortune's model of justice-making has been recognised as an authentic and healing way for organisations to deal with complaints of abuse/harassment:

- Truth-telling

- Acknowledgement of the truth and the wrong done

- Compassion for the victim

- Protection of the vulnerable (willingness to balance power in favour of the less powerful)

- Accountability – by perpetrator

- Restitution – willingness by perpetrator to make up for wrong

- Vindication

    - bringing the victim's story into the life of the community

    - possibility of ritual or sacramental healing

- Restoration – willingness to assist victim's restoration to their place in the church/workplace/community.

These are the principles being aimed at in New Zealand church procedures. Awareness is growing that being re-abused by a complaints process has been a significant risk for complainants in the past. It is heartening to see the energy, experience and sensitivity that is now being accumulated on this painful topic, which is being used for the service and healing of those members of the Body of Christ who have been harmed by its ministers. There is much to be learned – a good start has been made!

Of Poppies and Vines... 1997

Northern Italy in the early summer, Pentecost Sunday to be precise. Sunny and warm, zipping along on our luxury coach, almost non-stop between Vienna and Venice. Asking Alessandro our driver to slow down so I could take a photo when we got to the River Piave. My grandfather fought in a battle there in 1918, and won a Military Medal for bravery. I'd known about it for years, but had never dreamed that I'd actually visit the place. So at the right moment we slowed and through the bus window I took a shot of the wide, ice-green, tranquil-looking river. Hard to reconcile that scene with warfare, violence and death. Sitting down, wondering what it was like for young Will and his companions here, back then, in a bitter battle that wiped out most of his regiment. At 24 he'd had to take command of the remnant.

A trip to Europe followed on from the Sydney Conference – a wonderful experience which included returning to my birthplace for the first time in 44 years, and this Pentecost insight, which came in the area of Italy where my grandfather had fought in World War I.

A sudden shock as we passed a field stained red with poppies. Through history and poetry and Anzac Day services the connection between war and poppies and blood and Flanders was in me. But this was Italy, and here it was again – unlooked for, very personal. As we travelled south we'd seen smatterings of poppies, sometimes under the martialed rows of poplars, sometimes in a field, highlighting the tapestry of buttercups and Queen Anne's lace. This was a solid carpet, like a bloodstain. But very beautiful. Poppies for remembrance. Any pinned-on poppies I see now will have the memory of that river and that field trailing as a cloud of glory around them.

Vineyards became a frequent sight. The tour guide informed us that: vines are grown higher in Italy than in France and Germany. There the warmth from the ground is needed for adequate growth. In Italy, as in New Zealand, the sun provides sufficient warmth. The twisted trunks each with its two main branches trained horizontally were distinctly visible. A tall stake for each rose some way over the cross-wire. There was something achingly familiar about that shape. I focussed on an individual vine in the seconds it took to pass, and with a catch of breath suddenly I saw the connection. It looked crucified! *I am the vine.* I knew without a shadow of a doubt that Jesus had seen vines at this stage of growth and had made the same connection. *I am the vine!*

This image too had suddenly gained a shocking new depth. *I am the vine and you are the branches.* Yes, there they were, growing young and straight up from the crucified arms, the first leaves out, full of potential. It would not be long until they too would need to be bound to the horizontal. Without training and support they would not be able to bear the weight of the fruit, as the sap rose through the vine and recreated the ancient cycle. The vine-dresser would secure and tend the vine. *I am the vine.* This stretched-out shape of life that looked so much like the stretched-out shape of death. *You are the branches.* You too will be trained and pruned and shaped. The Vine-dresser will tend you as he tends me, so that the times that look and feel like deaths will be the times of rising sap and promise of new life, new fruit. As my crucifixion bore fruit so will yours. *I am the vine…*

Did Jesus, looking at the cruciform vine, carry with him the image of new shoots rising from its arms as he approached his death? Did the disciples at the Last Supper 'get the picture' as he offered them the image? They were a motley lot of fishermen and tax collectors, not viticulturists. Or maybe it was the next spring when John and the others stopped in their tracks at the sight of a knobbly-kneed trunk and branches spread like nailed arms, and shoots of new life springing up. Then they knew what he meant when he'd said *I am the vine and you are the branches.*

And the poppies became the blood of crucifixion. And young men dying included Jesus. And the women who wept included my grandmother and all the millions of others. My being there to honour lives and deaths was a part of resurrection. And God spoke through the poppies and the vines …

Life

Now comes the dancing
After dark storm times
Traumas and their consequences
Comes rainbow time
Freedom in sunshine
New beginnings
A sense of being
In the world
Within the companionship
Of those who have also
Been in deep
And come through the ordeal
Life in the light
Beckons, invites
Nothing can touch me now
Is probably an overstatement
More accurately
If I can survive all that
I can survive anything

Although the abuse experience was not over (that hope had been dashed so often), another window of thinking appeared: at least it was survivable, and there was some hope for an okay future.

Seeing

Today
The sky turned red
The ground fell away
And I left suspended
In the web
Saw the black and hairy feet
Of those who
Passed me round
And wound the parcel round
From one to another
Then on to the next
Helpless
Paralysed
Set up as victim
Donated as such
As the first defended the next
– and the next.
What am I going to do?
Stay away?
Or flail and kick
And create such chaos
That this web too will be
Holed beyond repair.
It is so bizarre
That the last who began so much
Now rails at consequences
The obvious is invisible
Justice and pain non-events
Power-broking their culture
I'll have none of it
None!
Not now not ever
I'm on the right track
My track
And that's where I stay
Feet now grounded
A dawn of sorts ahead.

As I had become more
engaged with my
psychotherapy, there were
moments of horror as
I began understanding
what had put me at risk
of being abused. And
recognising the patterns
of patriarchal self-defence
in the way my complaint
had been handled.

Outrage

Christa, woman
Dear friend, my sister
They crucified you too
Bound you and nailed you
With lying words
Words that just don't fit
The reality
Of our made-by-Godness
Why when there was already
More pain than enough
Did the church
Not heal, save, protect
And even build you up
As a beautiful spotless soul
In whom our God delights?
Instead the bruised reed
Was well and truly crushed
The flickering flame
Almost extinguished
Saved only by the will
To survive and God-breath
No credit at all to those who
Claim the power of righteousness

I rage for you
And all our crucified sisters
I rage at power abused
Behind fronts of Godly garb
I rage at all the pain
Inflicted by men on women
Since the beginning
And I thank Jesus crucified
For joining us
For coming to see what it was like
And becoming part
Of the whole sordid mess
Not that that makes it okay

Just now we know
God knows what its like
So we can claim in that Name
Our truth, God's justice
And some credit
For our challenge to the church

And then there was
Or rather is
The Resurrection
Which signals something
Has to come of it

So your story split my heart in two
And hauled guts up my throat
To become flames of fury
Flames of fight
God, purify your church
And heal your women
Bring us back from our graves
Teach us joy
And for Christa's sake
Sort out your men!

A Theology of Forgiveness

We know Christians are 'supposed' to forgive. It is what we expect of ourselves and others who have been injured. In the words of the familiar hymn – 'It is in forgiving that we're forgiven.' So understanding its practicalities in the painful experiences of our lives is crucial. But is it really so simple?

> The matter of forgiveness is important when there have been significant injuries. When is it morally appropriate? Could I – should I – forgive? How? How much?

For forgiveness to be necessary, there has to have been an injury, occurring within a context or relationship. Injuries cause distress from slight to severe; they can be isolated, repeated or constant; with effects that are brief to lifelong. The degree of intentionality varies: was it accidental, or fully and consciously malicious? A stranger steps on your toe in a bus and apologises. Most would find forgiveness easy here. A child accidentally breaks a treasured vase. It saddens, but is unlikely to wreck the relationship. A drunk driver kills a teenage son. Now we are getting into the tough areas. A man finally talks about being sexually abused as a boy. Do we recommend prompt Christian forgiveness here? A husband beats his wife three or four times a week. Is she really supposed to forgive seventy-times-seven?

What is the outcome of forgiveness? How can we tell whether we've 'done it'? There is a spectrum of possibilities. At one end, there can be total restoration of the previous loving relationship, or indeed its strengthening. This is what we need from our God, and it can happen between human beings. But there are many Christian people who, as well carrying ongoing pain and trauma, have an extra load of guilt because, despite desperate attempts to do so, they are unable or unwilling to forgive in this way. It may be just too dangerous – physically, emotionally, mentally or spiritually. Perhaps what our gentle God asks of them is simply an eventual desire to not bear a grudge, rather than doing further violence to themselves by forcing reconciliation. This is forgiveness too!

I believe urgings to forgiveness have been misused by the church, unwittingly or otherwise, asa patriarchal tool to prevent social analysis and change. Until very recently, women who mentioned domestic violence in the confessional were urged 'to forgive and try harder.' Who gained? Certainly not the victims! 'Forgiveness' and returning to the relationship aborted any hope of justice, or even safety. It took the secular world to produce the healing 'Good News' of Women's Refuges and Rape Crisis Centres, and to highlight the reality of the cycle of violence and 'reconciliations.' No wonder they list the church among the 'institutional supports for battering'!

Living in safety, and maintaining or regaining one's dignity as a child of God are basic human rights. God did not urge the enslaved Hebrews to forgive the Egyptians – Moses was called to challenge oppression, to lead them out of Egypt to a land of freedom. Sadly, I have listened to many women in violent relationships who have not heard this Good News. They have only heard that turning the other cheek and forgiving seventy-times-seven are what God and the church require of them. Yet it is 'obvious' to most that this cannot really be what God wants. How to resolve this conflict between scriptural injunctions and 'normal' common sense?

A key is found in The Kairos Document (1985), issued by a group of South African theologians in the apartheid era: 'Biblical teaching on reconciliation and forgiveness makes it quite clear that nobody can be forgiven and reconciled with God unless he or she repents of their sins. Nor are we expected to forgive the unrepentant sinner … As disciples of Jesus we should … promote truth, justice and life at all costs, even at the cost of creating conflict and disunity ….' Repentance means redressing any power imbalance and demonstrating lived change, not simply apologies and promises. Only then, if at all, is restoration of a relationship even a possibility.

Accountability, justice and prevention must be considered. New Zealanders were moved when the Tongan community forgave the Samoan driver who had killed one of their children. It was surely deeply healing to the young man. Nevertheless, he was still required to pay the official legal penalty.

A friend of mine, believing it was 'the Christian thing to do,' many years ago 'forgave' the relative who sexually abused her young son, on his assurance it would never happen again, and chose not to involve the police. When she occasionally met the perpetrator she gave him a family kiss, despite her revulsion at what he had done. She has since agonised over what seemed like her share of responsibility for this man later abusing several other children. Not for another fifteen years did he have to face up to the justice system and prison. In rational terms, of course, she is not responsible. As his serial offending demonstrated, initial reporting may not have protected other children. Her anger has finally surfaced, and is now directed not only at the abuser, but at the church from which she had heard no alternative framework to deal with this sort of scenario. 'Forgiveness' and 'reconciliation' without justice, or where repeat offending is likely or possible, are simply counter-productive. They do not further the reign of justice and compassion!

Our Maker knows all about the intricacies of human-being-ness. We are learning more. As research into trauma progresses, we are discovering more about what is genuinely healing to victims of injury and abuse. Unfortunately many such people have been further damaged by well-meaning Christians urging forgiveness as the solution to problems experienced after an injury. These are then compounded by the victim's guilt at not being able to forgive; or by straining at premature forgiveness by denying damage and pain, and suppressing appropriate anger. This can produce a worse state than before. Often in church circles the expectation is voiced that victims of sexual abuse, including that perpetrated by clergy, 'should' eventually forgive their abusers. This community-imposed 'spiritual' agenda can, however, actually impede the healing.

It is imperative that the human processes involved in healing from trauma be acknowledged in church teaching, for example, in Sunday sermons. Simplistic teaching on the necessity for Christian forgiveness can mean people leave Sunday worship more burdened than they came. In a recent homily: 'If they haven't forgotten, they haven't forgiven'!!! But it is neither possible nor appropriate to forget the traumas of our lives; to have further burdens laid on us for remembering ('and therefore not forgiving') is not

God's healing way. Our faith is built on remembering – 'Do this in memory of me.' We must remember tendencies to serial crimes and the crucifixions of war, of the Holocaust, to break patterns and to experience authentic resurrections.

Desperately trying to forget is not a healthy option: we have to establish accountability, see justice done, and to work through our pain and anger before considering whether it is safe, possible or even desirable to resume or restore a relationship. The task may simply be learning to live without bitterness and vindictiveness – for these corrode the heart, mind and body. God wants us healed of damage inflicted on us by others. As part of that process, which may be long, we will surely be guided by the Spirit of Truth and Compassion to an eventual release of the perpetrator into God's hands, without doing further violence to ourselves.

Forgiveness, then, varies in its outcome, and is likely to be a process rather than an event. It is a delicate plant, to be gently nurtured, not forced. When and if conditions are right, it will flower in its right season! Until then, God's healing is to be found in being gentle with ourselves.

Discovering Decolonisation

I went in July 1998 to the 'Breaking the Boundaries Conference' in Melbourne, dealing with sexual abuse by clergy and health professionals. I went as both a professional and as a survivor.

Decolonisation was not a word that sparked any ideas for me when designated as the topic for an edition of *Vashti's Voices*, the feminist theology journal. Then an uncomfortable experience I had at the second Australasian Conference on Sexual Abuse by Clergy and Health Professionals found its word – and I recognised my own bi-cultural understanding had been moved along.

At the conference there were many good, talented, experienced people who for various reasons have chosen to work in this painful area. Without them and their accumulated wisdom, the journey to healing for those they help would undoubtedly be more difficult. But during the first day I became uncomfortable as I heard a social worker talk about 'my' support group, as the presence at the conference of a number of survivors did not seem to be getting acknowledged, as professionals talked to professionals 'over' or 'about' us. I had a sense of a developing industry, with some of those who work in the field becoming somewhat proprietorial in delivering their undoubtedly valuable contributions. And then the word arrived in my mind. I felt colonised! – and said so at the plenary session the first afternoon.

I asked that power of naming the experience be left with survivors, to those who have had it. Then offered as a model New Zealand's 'Violence Intervention Programmes' (VIPs) philosophy of ensuring that the women who have been subjected to domestic violence are overtly recognised as the reference point of all the work, all the programmes, all the policies. They recognise within VIPs in New Zealand that returning power in every possible way to those who have experienced the extremes of powerlessness is the answer to 'How do we help them heal? Not advice, but education, offering language, and invitation to collective action as in Paulo Freire's educational framework. Utterly and respectfully insistent on the women's ownership of their own healing and decision-making!

A brief splatter of applause, then someone said it was a pity to set up a 'them and us situation.' In that moment I knew the acrid taste of dis-empowerment by colonisation. I had, apparently, created an unwelcome polarisation by speaking my truth. Whose job, I wondered, was it to heal that breach? Were survivors supposed to accommodate yet again, to be quiet and let the experts get on with their business?

It got worse: on the fourth day, the conference organisers, good and dedicated people, launched a project to provide ongoing spiritual and emotional support for both victims (choice of word noted!) and those who work in the field. As part of the launch, a man they had flown in from out of town spoke of how helpful they had been to him. But then as he began recounting appalling details of his ritual abuse by a priest, the conference organiser called to him across the hall, 'No, M …, no!.' So he stopped, floundered a little, finished his talk, and shortly afterwards left the room. This incident left me and others in shock. Someone who had been so brutally silenced during his years of abuse had just been silenced yet again by the very people who were supposed to be helping him! Maybe, if he were in such a fragile state that there might be inappropriate disclosure of detail, the worse colonisation was in having him there at all.

There were other instances during the four days of conference, and in scriptural good order they have been addressed with the people concerned. A number of people have offered feedback, because a healthy organisation must always be ready for critique geared towards a better outcome for the people who are the focus of their assistance.

What I have drawn from this experience is a deep knowing of an unwitting lack of respect from 'helpers,' which at a conference like this of all places should not have been evident. Now I know for sure that decolonisation is to do with me and other survivors!

- It is to do with claiming a voice, with breaking the silence, with refusing to be silenced yet again.

- It is to claim the right to name sexual abuse by clergy and health professionals as sexual abuse should we so choose, rather than as sexual misconduct or sexual exploitation.

- It is to insist on the right to heal in the way that becomes apparent to each of us, and to resist well-intentioned efforts at taking over the process (for example, church pressures to forgive).

- It is to invite the New Zealand organisers of the next such conference in two-years' time to ensure that their fundamental philosophy is survivor-centred, and that this is modelled within the conference dynamics.

Nevertheless, many wonderfully good and useful things were said and done in Melbourne. A highlight for me was Reverend Patricia Allan's magnificent meditation on Mother Church as the woman with the haemorrhage. It was a plea for humility by the church. And balm was unexpectedly poured in the wound of feeling colonised by two men who have listened and understood. A Trappist priest used a story from the Grail legends about a wounded king who could not be healed unless a question was asked. The knight Parzival had to go through many tribulations and much learning before he developed enough mature humility and compassion to ask, 'What are you going through?' That question of itself, and the willingness to hear the answer, were what healed. And what still heal!

Catholic Bishop Geoffrey Robinson of Sydney, when speaking on the spiritual damage caused by sexual abuse, used spirituality in its widest possible sense – the loves which give meaning to our lives. 'Sexual abuse is a bulldozer gouging a road through a fragile eco-system of meanings.' And, he said, he has discovered that the way he is very often able to be useful to survivors is to help them leave the church as comfortably as possible, because healing for many simply is not possible in a church context. I felt a physical relief on hearing that, as though he had lifted a weight from my back. He has listened well, and reflected humbly and honestly.

That attitude I can now name as decolonisation!

- It is the will, the decision, to serve by listening.

- It is making a space for the perspective of those who have been disempowered, as they find their unique way to heal.

- It is defending and safeguarding their inner wisdom, while resisting urges to override and control it with a corporate agenda or party-line.

- It frees people to be themselves.

- It is refraining from thinking one knows best, and about fostering self-determination!

As a British immigrant, it took me quite a long time to develop a realisation of and sense of communal guilt for what England did to Māori, to Indians, to the Irish and others, even while intellectually acknowledging the evils of colonisation. Those few days in Melbourne have given me an experiential understanding of the word I could never have acquired from workshops or movies! Hopefully, as a result, I will become increasingly sensitised to issues of power and control in my dealings with others.

A Letter

Dear Jesus

There are a few things puzzling and intriguing me, so I thought I'd run them past you.

The fascination with the inter-play between religious faith and human wholeness continued. A wonderful image for this is the double helix of DNA, where the connectors hold the two 'aspects' together.

You related to people who came your way with such respect. Often you anticipated their needs before they'd had a chance to tell you what they were. Often they came, not even sure what to ask for, because the whole problem was just too much. And you dealt with them in ways beyond what they'd dared to dream. I don't suppose it had crossed the mind of the mother of the young man on her way to his burial to hope you'd bring him back to life. But you did it anyway. What I'm seeing is that your boundless capacity to bless and surprise us isn't altogether limited by our faith or vision or lack thereof. You can simply be moved by compassion and produce moments of astonishment. I think that's what Jung called synchronicity. Does it matter too much what they are called – as long as they are noticed and savoured?

Jung was convinced that the spiritual dimension was the key to almost all the emotional and psychological problems of his patients. He also introduced us to the world of archetypes. Those shadowy but immensely powerful images who inhabit the deep realms within each of us, inviting and challenging us to greater wholeness – to the abundant life that you promised to give us. When I read a book about archetypes the list made for profound thought: the divine child, the creator, the magician, the joker/trickster, the saviour, the lover, the care-giver, the wise king and others. What really intrigued me was the thought that all these archetypes are somehow or other found in you, in the stories we have about your life on earth, in the titles we give you. Is this the real significance of your 'laying down your life' and your Divinity? That in and through you we are able to access whatever archetypes we need to become complete? When you come in prayer to startle and heal, is this the same phenomenon that is experienced by those who simply encounter the archetypes, say, in their dreams?

And another thing – that stuff about your Heavenly Father sending you 'down' to earth to die: any human mother, and I suspect human father too, must, if they really think about it, choke on the thought – I have even heard it called Divine child abuse. What makes sense to me is the reality that challenges to powerful establishments, and uncompromising stands for truth and justice, inevitably attract crucifixion. It happened before you were born. It happened to you. It continues to happen today. This is the miracle and hope of the Resurrection: that truth and justice are ultimately going to triumph, that they are like the phoenix that arises from the ashes of the fire in which their opponents have sought to dispose of them; or like the flame of those silly birthday cake candles which can only be extinguished in the short term… then leap back to life again, seemingly by magic.

And another thing, Jesus, why is it, when you deliberately chose not just to visit and honour with your presence the marginalised people of your time, but to actually become one of them – to be totally and utterly marginalised yourself – that this model is not often visible in your church? There's an impression often given that the church consists of 'us, the okay people' who have a lot to offer the 'you, the not-okay people.' When 'you' become like 'us' then you too will be okay. And sometimes there's a none-too-hidden agenda – we'll be really nice to people, so that they will see the light and become like us. Is that what you meant to happen, a sort of seductive colonising? Or are we supposed to affirm people for who they already are? Because I have a hunch that that is the sort of acceptance that really heals and saves. That's how you dealt with all you met. The real Good News was that you had become aware of their existence, you acknowledged them with respect, cared enough about their pain to do something about it. 'You matter, you matter to me!' was your message. I think this is what every human heart needs to hear. How are we doing in continuing your work?

I'll be expecting an answer, Jesus. Help me be alert to the whispers and breezes.

Love
Trish

Trinity

I was quite small when I first met, so to speak, the Blessed Trinity. Six or seven, probably, and in the Penny Catechism. 'How many Persons are there in God?' 'There are three persons in God.' 'Who are the three persons in God?' 'The three persons in God are the Father, the Son, and the Holy Spirit, known as the Blessed Trinity.' 'How can we understand the Blessed Trinity?' 'We cannot understand the Blessed Trinity – this is a mystery of our Faith.'

Could this Mystery still have relevance to my evolving belief system? Track the stories, re-examine, reframe!

'Don't tangle with this' was the message. That would be a sin of arrogant presumption. The Trinity is out there somewhere. Just believe it! No answers this side of heaven. And so the theory was instilled. You can't understand It but believe It anyway. That was Tertullian's[17] 'one substance, three persons.'

As an adult reading theology, trying to make experiential sense of this religion of mine (because if I didn't, what was the use of it all?) I met the Augustinian[18] explanation. God the Father, the First Person of the Blessed Trinity, knew himself so profoundly that the Son, the Second Person of the Blessed Trinity, was generated by/from this knowledge from all eternity, and eventually became man in the person of Jesus. And, the story went, the love between the Father and the Son was so intense that this 'became' the Holy Spirit, the Third Person of the Blessed Trinity. A Community of three consubstantial co-equal Persons bound together in one will by their mutual love. It all sounded logical enough, even if I didn't feel it had very much to do with me.

Then came a period of metaphors. Most folk have heard of St Patrick's sermon on the Trinity, using a shamrock leaf to illustrate the message of three distinct persons with one shared life. Into my ponderings around this came other images. How about a plait of three gold threads – three in one, just like they said, and one strand looped down to thread the beads of our hollow humanity and bind us into the being of the Godhead. I was quite proud of that one! Less fanciful was the image of the three forms of H2O: I could equate the Father with water, as the essence and giver of all life, the Spirit with steam: aery, unfathomable breath, ever present, but only visible on frosty mornings. And Jesus, well, he was the ice. No analogy is perfect, and I had to disregard the temperature of a block of ice. But he was the holdable, touchable, solid form of God. 'Something which has existed since the beginning … which we have touched with our own hands.' (1 John 1:1)

During a lengthy charismatic phase I learnt to pray to all three members of the Trinity in different ways. It certainly felt more even-handed than giving one of them, or even two all the attention. The indwelling Spirit, received in baptism we were now told, not simply at confirmation, was invited to manifest His power in our lives. And He did – in ways that were sometimes awesome in their intensity, with physical sensations on occasion that shocked my faith into a new dimension. This God was too close, and far more involved in the nitty-gritty of our lives than I had ever imagined!

Later I came to understand the Spirit as the feminine principle of God, a role hitherto reserved for Mary. But with the post-Vatican II theological developments, she found herself firmly back in the human race. I can only imagine her relief! Given the Father and the Son, there just had to be Somebody somewhere in whose image I was made! And all those wonderful 'feminine' gifts of the Spirit – now returned to sender, so to speak – the 'love, joy, peace, patience, kindness, goodness, trustfulness, gentleness and self control.' It was obvious to me that the Spirit was indeed She. I began to get very uptight when I heard the Spirit referred to as He, and also when I realised that yet-another generation of little girls was learning subliminally through the language of the mass that God is 'like them' and 'not like us.'

Later again, as I was becoming disillusioned with the male God as presented by the church, Sandra Schneiders' description of the Trinity as 'more than two men and a bird' touched a deep chord. Theologically, clergy I talked to were really ready to admit that God was beyond gender, but many were fixated on how saying 'She' would be just as inaccurate. This ignored altogether the problem of the inaccuracy of 'He.' Why should one inaccuracy be used 97 percent of the time? That is just the way it is! I honour those who see, understand and make the effort.

An exultant 'YES' to Jim Cotter's original naming in his magnificent reworking of The Lord's Prayer: Life-giver, Pain-bearer, Love-maker. And to the somewhat censored version used in the Anglican Church's *A New Zealand Prayer Book:* Earth-maker, Pain-bearer, Life-giver. That felt like getting somewhere.

Elizabeth Johnson's book, *She Who Is*, filled a great hunger – a work of profound thealogical/theological significance, describing a God with whom women can feel as one, as men must be able to do with the Father; a recognition that all God-language is of necessity metaphor. As Thomas Aquinas said, 'If you think you have understood God, what you have understood is not God.'

And then this year, a researcher who has been exploring the spiritual journeys of many New Zealanders asked me that most deceptively simple of questions: 'How do *you* know there's a God? How do you know there is a God?' How indeed? And the experiences of over half a century, a kaleidoscopic cloud of witnesses whirled around me, and settled into a shape that I could begin to put into words. I know there's a God when I look at the stars, at a silver snail-trail in the morning sun, and at the self-sown white lily flowering amidst my red carpet rose. That is transcendence. I know there's a God when I look within, and Someone is bringing wholeness, giving strength, leaping joyously in whatever creativity I discover, and according to the promise in John 16, leading me into all truth. That is immanence. I know God in my relationships. God is love. God 'happens' when I cry and someone holds me, when I laugh with a friend, when our compassion is stirred for each other or someone else. That is the God between.

That's – that's three ways – wait a minute – why does that sound familiar? Could there be some trinitarian connection? A Re-worded Trinity? Is that what it is? Easy enough to see the Creator connection – then the Spirit at work within, in Quaker language, the Inner Light, 'that of God in everyone.' And yes, there is my Friend Jesus at work in and through others, affirming, encouraging, present in the deaths and resurrections of our lives just as he was in the gospel stories. A flood of recognition, of relief! Maybe the Blessed Trinity is not so mysterious after all! 'I am the Way, the Truth and the Life.' Is that the most profound trinitarian statement of them all? The actuality of where we are, how we are and who we are – all inextricably interwoven with God-presence.

Oh my God! Oh my, God! Oh, *my* God! It was one of those extraordinary homecoming moments described so succinctly by T S Eliot in 'Little Gidding'[12]:

> 'And the end of our exploring
> Will be to arrive where we started
> And know the place for the first time.'

Then I was able to name the different approaches as the old 'descending theology' and the newer 'ascending theology.' It depends which end of the telescope you look through! And a sadness! Knowing God, and knowing that we know God is our birthright. These are such simple ways that we can begin to recognise the God who is so intimately concerned with each one of us. Why did they make it sound so complicated?

'Come and See!'

A weekend for enquirers was held at the Settlement in Wanganui over Labour Weekend. A dozen or so enquirers joined several experienced Friends and six Friends who had put together a programme for a special encounter. We came from a variety of belief backgrounds, and from as far apart as Christchurch and Auckland. Many diverse threads, and by the end of the weekend we had been woven together into a new sort of a pattern, thanks to the skilful facilitation, and drawn by the unity experienced in the silence of worship. This worship was the ground and the essence of the experience. From that flowed the rest!

The Quaker emphasis on the principles of truth, simplicity, non-violence and equality for all, rather than on doctrinal belief, had a strong appeal for me. It was a good match as I shed what I now experienced as clutter. I am grateful for the experience of being part of that community for seven years.

This was my first visit to the Settlement. Its tranquillity and welcoming beauty, not to mention the comfortable bunks and food, glorious food, gave us a great base from which to open ourselves to everything that was offered. The Friday night enabled us to give our own flavour to the agenda: what were the questions and expectations we'd come with? They ranged from the huge (where is Quakerism going?) to the practical (what are the conditions/obligations of membership?) with many in between. Several Friends presented their perspectives on key aspects of Quaker life and worship, which were followed up by discussions and more questions. All very enlightening!

There are many powerful impressions: awe at being able to actually hold the book published in 1671. That's right, the year George Fox left on his mission to North America! It is a tribute to the life and death of James Parnell, an early Quaker. Did George Fox read this very same book on his return? Whatever, it has been lovingly passed down through the generations to its present home on the other side of the world. It summed up for me the sense of Quaker love for their history, for telling their stories, for acknowledging their roots. This was present too on our 'tour' of the selection of Quaker Tapestry panels in the dining room. I'd seen the originals in Kendal (UK) in 1996 – before I had any inkling that I might move in a Quaker direction. Circle-dancing and singing were the evening pleasures – Taizé chants around the fire another memorable moment.

A learn-by-doing experience was provided by the enquirers conducting their own meeting for business, with guidance and minimal coaching from the others. The task was to arrive at an agreed agenda/format for the Monday morning session to cover the questions that had not been explored as fully as we wished. To have a discussion held within, as we were told, a meeting for worship, was a good experience – respectful, open, with a shared positive expectation of the right outcome. Communal discernment, I would call it, and I noted similarities to Rogerian and Zen group process.

We, or at least I, learned some new words, and new (Quaker) meanings to old ones: birthright, convincement, 'speak to your condition,' testimony. This latter in many

Christian contexts means the personal story of someone's own conversion/enlightenment. In Quaker-speak it seems to mean something approaching a creed. The 17th century usages can be a little obscure and confusing, but certainly add to the flavour. Does this help or hinder a 21st century New Zealander in reaching the essence of the life-style? Mainstream churches have adopted current usages in the last 30 years or so to reduce the language barrier.

Another comment from an uninformed perspective: the common perception that Quakers have neither ritual nor dogma was thoroughly disposed of during the weekend! These may be different in shape and dimension from those in mainstream Christianity, but they are there all right! While theology is not a Quaker-favoured word, my Catholic-formed meaning for it is 'faith seeking understanding'; and in that sense Quakers are aiming to 'do theology' consistently through the whole of their lives. Which is impressive!

So there were many questions answered, and others have emerged since. But the most important aspect of the weekend was the experience of how Quakers 'be and do' together, and hearing a range of perspectives from those who gave their time to help us increase our knowledge and understanding. Thanks to everyone for a memorable weekend. With the awareness of 'that of God' in us all, it's great to have some new F/friends. And to have been able to explore in more depth the gift-question of one speaker: 'Are these the people among whom I want to do my seeking?'

Engaging with the Scriptures   *1999*

As will have been apparent, my early engagement with the Bible as a book, as God's inspired Word, took place in the context of my charismatic covenant community, Lamb of God. I regard the teaching now as a somewhat fundamentalist approach, but because it was in a Catholic context it was never a 'Scripture alone' framework. Catholicism has always held that Scripture and Tradition inform each other. It was more a selective literalism, for example, re male headship, expectation of miracles. I got to know the Bible fairly well during this period of some 16 years. What awed me then and still does now is God's way of highlighting or referring me to sometimes unknown texts to show the way, for example, the Susanna story. Telling the stories of our own God-experiences seems to me to be a way of continuing the theme of the Bible as a record of God's action in the lives of human beings.

This was part of my application to be recognised as an Associate in Christian Ministry by The New Zealand Association of Theological Schools.

Several eight-day retreats (1985-1995) meant that I was immersed in the Ignatian spirituality method of taking verses and interacting with them, and using feeling responses as a basis for prayer. This continues to be fruitful.

Reading Elisabeth Schuessler Fiorenza's *In Memory of Her*, about 1992, was an eye-opener. I met the phrase the 'hermeneutics of suspicion,' learned to wonder about the women's stories, and recognised the influence of patriarchy on both the writing and the interpretation of Scripture.

Introductory Theology ('find all available relevant Scriptures') and Old Testament Women courses ('find a story to interact with') at the Catholic Education Centre were very influential. We were introduced to the concept of the gospels as being written with the hindsight of the Resurrection. This made a lot of sense but required some re-thinking: I'd been taught Jesus was proven to be the Messiah because of the 330-odd ways he fulfilled Old Testament prophecies (for example, in *More than a Carpenter*, Josh McDowell). It was quite a leap to accept that the stories of these 'fulfilments' were written into the gospels because the evangelists wished to demonstrate their post-Resurrection beliefs about Jesus. In a Theology of Mary course, reflection was encouraged on whether personal faith is based on/affected by literal understandings of the infancy narratives, for example, the virginity of Mary. And no, mine isn't. There is Truth conveyed by both newspaper reports and poems, and understanding Scripture as closer to poem than newspaper makes more sense. These learnings have ultimately led to discomfort with much of the church style and liturgical presentation.

Sister Sandra Schneiders' two-day workshop 'God is more than Two Men and a Bird' on the feminist perspective of the New Testament (1997) was exciting – confirming much I already knew, but expanding it further. Bishop John Spong's lectures (1998) gave me more of a sense of the Jewish context in which the Scriptures were written and how they have been largely interpreted in a European understanding. I was particularly intrigued with his correlation of the Jewish liturgical year with Matthew's gospel. I respect the rigorous intellectual honesty of Lloyd Geering and others. It is a totally necessary exploration, but I wonder whether taken on its own, this ground-up approach is not another manifestation of Western male rationalism – there seems to be no sense of the experience of the numinous in their considerations!

I am aware of and interested in the work of the Jesus Seminar, but I do not find it personally relevant. I have a relationship with the Jesus who has intervened in my life in many ways. Albert Nolan's *Jesus Before Christianity* describes the Man I know.

The internet yielded a gem recently – a very convincing argument that it was actually Mary Magdalene who wrote John's gospel, based on the work of Raymond Brown, a well-respected Catholic Scripture scholar.

Through my counselling and spiritual direction training and work, I have come in recent years to recognise the power exerted by symbol, myth, metaphor and story-telling on the human psyche. My feeling now is that the Bible is a rich and privileged source of all these, which can work in our lives to promote meaning, hope and healing. The prime example is the Death and Resurrection story.

All this makes for a more, rather than less, awesome God! But one less connectable with standard Sunday worship!

Journey with the Jews

Some reflection on my journey with regard to the Jews, the Chosen People, has been prompted recently by reading in *Tui Motu InterIslands*[20] of the pain caused them by the lack of an apology by Pope John Paul II for the church's inadequate stance against Nazi Germany; and more recently by the canonisation of Edith Stein who became a Catholic Christian, and a Carmelite nun who was killed in Auschwitz, offering her death for 'our unbelieving people.' There has also been discussion in *The Tablet* (London) around this, and a crass dismissal of Jewish expression of pain by a Vatican official. What are we to make of all this? I have searched my own stories and found what may be some clues.

Having Jewish friends, and being conscious of our shared history and Book, provided the impetus to review my changing perspectives on the interface between Judaism and Christianity. This journey continued with a pilgrimage in 2003 to Jewish sites in Eastern Europe.

I have an early memory of asking my mother what 'perfidious' meant. That was how Jews were described in our Good Friday bidding prayers. Whatever her response, the word is unpleasant and demeaning. It was a relief to have it dropped from the ceremonies in the post-Vatican II move towards interfaith respect. And there was a story I read about a small Jewish boy who was beaten up by some Gentile yobs and taunted with the word 'kike.' He had gone home and asked his mother what a 'kike' was, and she told him it meant a Christ-killer. Not surprisingly, that added bewilderment to the blood and bruises. I cried for him and the unfairness of it all. Nonetheless, pictures of the liberation of the death camps at the end of World War II somehow fused these images together in my child mind – if they were, as the church said, 'perfidious,' then maybe some of these ghastly things were somehow deserved.

The issue faded from consciousness till well into adult life when I became acquainted with the Old Testament (now known as the Hebrew Scriptures) as the book which foretold the Messiah, the Christ. My prayer group, later a covenant community, felt a unity with the Jewish faith heritage. We noted that many of the prayers of the mass were based on traditional Jewish bereka (prayers). 'Blessed are you, Lord God of all Creation ...' took on another dimension when we realised that we prayed this in common with our Jewish brethren.

We explored their rituals, and used an adapted form of the household ceremony to lead in our Sabbath. For them it is the ancient Friday night ceremony, where the mother of the household lights the candles and prays blessing on her family. Two loaves of bread, representing the tablets on which the commandments were given, are initially covered on the table. Later they are blessed and shared as each family member gives thanks for something. A cup of wine is also blessed and shared. With readings and prayers, thanks are given for the gift of the Sabbath itself, God's gift of re-creation. Then the age-old greeting, 'Shabat shalom!' – 'the peace of the Sabbath!'

For us as Christians, this was a Saturday night event to herald our Sunday-Sabbath. Several families joined together, and children and adults became familiar with our Jewish faith-roots. There was something deep and awesome in recognising that Mary of Nazareth would have lit the candles and prayed the same Kiddush prayer in her home as we women prayed for our families at these Sabbath meals.

As we grew familiar with the Old Testament stories, we explored the Jewish festivals based on the Book we have in common. There is Purim, to celebrate the rescue of the Jewish people by Queen Esther and her uncle Mordecai from the plot to eliminate them by the wicked Haman. There is Sukkot, the Feast of Tabernacles or booths, which like others was originally an agricultural observance, but became a commemoration of the time that Israel lived in tents in the desert. There is Passover, with the seder/meal where families re-enter the experience of the Exodus with food symbols and the retelling of the stories of the escape from Egypt. For how many Christians is this traditional meal a familiar and real context within which to hear the gospel stories of the Last Supper? On the table in that upper room would have been the lamb, the bitter herbs, the haroset, the salt water, the eggs – not simply the unleavened bread and wine of Leonardo da Vinci's painting.

Hannukah, the Feast of Lights, is when Jewish children receive their gifts, as those of Christian-based cultures do at Christmas. This feast celebrates the re-dedication of the Temple in 165 BC after the Maccabees had defeated the colonising Syrian Greeks. A book about these festivals gave me much pleasure as I recognise the correspondences with the familiar stories. But a comment on the customs for this feast caused my blood to run cold: American Jewish parents were encouraged to confine giving gifts to children to Hannukah, and not to conform to the prevailing culture by using Christmas. And then: 'Christmas celebrates the birth of the one they call the Prince of Peace. But his followers have meant anything but peace to our people for 2000 years.' I was stricken with an awareness that the Christian church and people have not been 'good news' to Jesus' own people. How could they possibly hear any proclamation of the Messiah, when appalling persecution has been meted out by the 'ambassadors for Christ,' at such regular intervals?

About that time I had a nightmare: I saw women and children being rounded up in front of the Bundestag where Hitler was making a speech. I woke in terror, knowing exactly what was going to happen next. I reached for my Bible as a way to ease my fear and tension. It opened at Psalm 22 (the psalm quoted by Jesus on the cross) – and did nothing to soothe: 'I am like water draining away, my heart is like wax melting inside me; my palate is drier than a potsherd and my tongue is stuck to my jaw. A pack of dogs surrounds me, a gang of villains closes me in; they tie me hand and foot and leave me lying in the dust of death. I can count every one of my bones, and there they glare at me gloating; they divide my garments among them and cast lots for my clothes.' And the images of the death camp prisoners coalesced with the familiar words.

Some German people still carry a sense of communal guilt about what their country did to fellow human beings during WWII. In the middle of that night I felt the weight of guilt for what Christians have done to Jews across the centuries, of which the Holocaust was an extreme, but by no means isolated example. So I was compelled to seek out my very few Jewish friends to say to them, 'I am just beginning to understand what we Christians have done to your people, and I am so sorry.'

As a church, as a Christian people, we have sinned. We have sinned both against the Jewish people, and against the good news-bearing Jew we know as Jesus. I would like the Pope to apologise to the Jews on behalf of us all, for the events of this and all the centuries of persecution. The term Christ-killer was introduced in third century of the Christian era and that is when Jews officially became the scapegoats for the Crucifixion. And did you know that in the Papal States in the 13th century they were made to wear yellow discs or shields as a mark of identification? Hitler was simply reviving an old Catholic practice …. The apology that is needed is not simply about Pius XII, or Vatican insensitivity around the canonisation of an apostatising Jew. It must be for the entirety of the church's initiation of, and scene-setting for, all Christian-based anti-semitism. We must begin to know their whole story of how we have treated them.

I would like Pope John Paul II and his advisers to take up their history books and track the black thread of anti-semitism to its source. Then perhaps they will realise, when they have understood the huge old context, why recent efforts at apology have hurt, and why honouring Edith Stein distresses.

In recent years I met Viktor Frankl's classic book, Man's Search for Meaning. He survived incarceration in Auschwitz, and as a psychologist himself reflected on what made survival possible. His conclusion that love is what gives meaning to life has inspired millions. He is a shining example of God's word in Zechariah 8 in our shared Testament '… those of nations of every language will take a Jew by the sleeve and say, "We want to go with you, since we have learnt that God is with you."' I affirm all moves to establish inter-faith respect and dialogue with those with whom we share so much. That they are still ready to speak with us, after all that, is in itself a miracle of grace! Can we do less than try to understand?

Revisiting Original Sin

More on the spirituality / psychology conjunction.

Do you remember learning that original sin was the stain of sin, Adam's sin that we were born with, which was removed by baptism? There was the corollary that baptism was when we were first filled with sanctifying grace, and got our passport to heaven, into which the unbaptised had no hope of entry. Original sin was the tendency to evil inherited from Adam, although it seems that Eve is the one who has actually carried the can.

My first doubts about this doctrine came when I observed my children growing up. They were, all six of them, loved, wanted, baptised before their first month was up – made heirs to the kingdom, had their original sin removed and were beautiful new creations. How come, I wondered, that baptised two year-olds could be just as revolting as unbaptised two year-olds, just as liable to tantrums and contrariness? 'Twas indeed a puzzle! Their being replete with baptismal grace did not actually seem to make an iota of practical difference. And there was of course my discovery of the tendencies to violence of various types within myself. They too had not been washed away by my own baptism. So I shelved the whole idea of original sin into the 'doubtful' box.

And gradually it seemed as if the church did too. Baptism was, in post-Vatican II times, redefined as one of the sacraments of initiation, that by which the child or adult is received into the community of the faith. Along the way I felt a leap of joy when I heard someone in the ministry of baptism preparation say she believes that babies are baptised in the waters of their mother's uterus. That is after all where the new person has his or her very first experience of community. So the external baptismal waters are an out-working of what has already taken place before birth.

That was the extent of the musings for many years, until I came across Matthew Fox's book, *Original Blessing*. He shone the spotlight onto the celebration of creation and away from the original sin. And the four paths of Creation Theology made a lot of sense. This solved for me the mystery of the apparently contradictory instructions on the spiritual life – the radical asceticism of St John of the Cross versus the earthy commonsense of Hildegard of Bingen *et al*. Once Fox had traced the strands of the two different traditions it all made more sense.

Two scholars have come my way recently who have each wrestled with the topic of original sin and come to conclusions that as far as I am concerned make sense in the 21st century.

The first was Neil Ormerod, an Australian Catholic lay theologian, who in his book, *Grace and Disgrace: A Theology of Self-esteem*, traces the history of the doctrine of original sin. This took him via the Augustinian view that all are born sinful because all conception is the result of concupiscence, through the gentler Thomistic position that what we lack is the grace to keep our nature in submission to reason.

He provides a convincing theoretical base for a modern understanding in the light of what we now know about the workings of the human psyche. His thesis is that original sin is what we experience as 'self-disesteem.' We are all born to imperfect (that is, human) parents who, as a result of their own wounds from their own imperfect parents, in their turn parent imperfectly, despite their best efforts and intentions.

Our childhood traumas in varying degrees leave their marks in lack of self-confidence, or excess thereof, in hunger for acceptance and inclusion, in efforts to compensate for probably unconscious perceptions of what was lacking in our early lives. And from these wounds come the unskilled behaviours we know as sin. The link between tragic childhoods and crime is only too well established. Ormerod sees baptism as the entry into a loving, accepting community where ideally those wounds can receive the necessary healings. We can discover that we are in fact lovable and acceptable in and through the parish community's love and acceptance, which mirror to us those of God.

Then, recently, I listened to Professor Heinrich Skolomowski, an eminent Polish scholar and eco-philosopher, as he set out his view in a series of lectures entitled 'The Journey of the Evolutionary God,' sponsored by the St Andrew's Trust, Wellington. His perspective is that just as the universe developed from the fragmenting caused by the Big Bang, and as an acorn has to split for an infant oak tree to develop roots and leaves, so all matter, human beings included, carries the imprint of this woundedness. He prefers to speak therefore of the Original Wound rather than Original Sin. The journey then for all that exists is one of healing and reconciling. This has its parallel in Colossians 1: 20: God's wanting 'all things to be reconciled through him (Christ) and for him, everything in heaven and everything on earth.'

Like so many of the former church teachings, original sin has been languishing, buried by the silt of time and irrelevance, but for me it has been a rich adventure to discover the efforts of these men, and to mine the concept for light-bearing nuggets to help us in our journeys of faith and hope.

Starting

To
See
That
I've
Been
Standing
Foot-bound
In
Jewelled
Shoes
On
The
Edge
Of
Life
Watching

While
Everyone else jumped
and danced and played
As they wished
Without thought
for where or how to tread

Is having a knife turned in my gut
What a waste!

To be root-bound
In a pot inside
Still able to
Flower but
Not to

flourish
and   put
down   roots
into   spacious
soil   is
not   enough
any   more

Dancing

Circle
Walking in a circle walking
In a circle walking in a circle
Connected
In touch and rhythm
Simply
One two three rock back
One two three rock back
Wheeling
Round still point
Of candle-glow
Silhouettes
Circling the ceiling
Eyes close in womb-like
Trance
Rocking rhythm
Connected pulsing
Sacred Life
And something
Darkly ancient
Knows I have been here
Before

God appears in
joyful moments of
Transcendence, often
not needing words.

Living Springs –
Towards a Just Future

A report on a
Feminist Theology
Conference.

If God is a verb, then when seventy or so women got
together last November to share their passion for the Big Questions, God Happened! I
came home on a high that lasted for weeks, which is still noticeable in a generally raised
energy level. It was being with all those women who, whatever else was going on in their
lives, set aside three days for playing, pondering, and praying (in its widest possible sense
of being in tune with ourselves and what is Beyond). Such wonderful energy, in the
laughter, in the way we worked with each other, in the collective wisdom, and generous
sharing of knowledge.

So many gems of experience that it's hard to choose! The purple ribbons to wear on the
plane; the warm welcome and kindly taxiing; Hildegard's presence among us as a woman
at home in the universe; the lesbian caucus's scintillating contribution to our spiritual
well-being at the concert; the earth, air, fire and water experiences of the opening and
closing liturgies – sparkler-stars and bubbles, an inspired blend of play and symbolism;
the explosiveness of compressed balloons – what happens when women get *really* close
to each other; the opportunity to present a workshop – a new experience for me with
a group that size – good learning; great net-working; being a 'dragon,' discovering ten
women can write a song over lunch, and that I can actually enjoy playing to an audience;
a new look at the telling of women's stories in the Hebrew Scriptures – how would Rahab
and Jezebel tell their own stories? *not like that!*; a phrase 'the eco-system of God' offered
as an improvement on 'the kingdom'; putting faces to names and getting a sense of the
strength and richness of woman-church nationwide; explaining to the lovely but surprised
young man in the office that, no, I do not believe Father God sent His Son to die for our
sins, and why; our honouring of the women who have attended these gatherings over the
last 20 years and the work they have done in the churches in the intervening years; the
sad saga of Conference of Churches of Aotearoa New Zealand; the Eucharist in the quiet
room – that astonishing view, and the redeeming of the apple as we shared a Granny
Smith and honey – 'the sharpness of God and the sweetness of God.'

That, as Eucharists are meant to do, summed it all up for me. The cutting edge of
women's thinking about God, church, and ourselves, about a Just Future, the pain of
struggle and encountering injustice and resistance. And the sweetness of new growth, the
respectful traditions of women-together, the tremendous gift the organising tri-feminate
gave us, the laughter, the shared energy for flourishing, and the acceptance of diversity –
wherever we are in our varying journeys, it's all fine!

All being well, the inner Living Springs will bubble away in each and every one of us for a
long time yet.

Open Discipline, Consumer Rights and the Churches

Looking at progress in accountability required by the community from professionals, and wondering that this same progress is resisted in churches…

Last year I cheered for Robyn Stent, the Health and Disability Commissioner, when she initiated an action (successful in theory at least: decision of 7 December 1998) through the High Court in an effort to get more open disciplinary processes by the Nursing Council. She also recommended publication of outcomes of disciplinary decisions by the Medical Council (*The Evening Post*, 18 September 1998). That was just before the annual report of the Medical Council was tabled in Parliament, listing simply as Doctors A, B, C, D and E those against whom charges of 'disgraceful conduct in a professional respect' had been heard. Despite charges against four of them being proven, two of these doctors were (are?) apparently still in practice (*The Evening Post*, 8 October 1998). We, patients or potential patients, do not know who they are. Stent then voiced her concerns that doctors may be covering up for unsafe colleagues (*Sunday Star-Times*, 11 October 1998).

The whole area of openness of discipline of unsafe practitioners, and publication of outcomes of complaints to protect consumer rights has become an issue for churches as well as for associations of medical professionals.

At the Melbourne Breaking the Boundaries Conference on sexual abuse by trusted professionals (health professionals, clergy etc) in July 1998, one of the guest speakers, Gary Schoener, commented that discipline without publication of its outcome was simply no use. Schoener is a US psychologist who has dealt with over three thousand cases of this type through the Walk-in Counseling Center, Minneapolis, where he is the Executive Director. He is also a member of the American Psychological Association's Task Force on Sexual Exploitation and the Impaired Psychologist, and has been an expert witness in many complaint hearings. While his comment was made about a more narrowly focussed spectrum of complaints (those of professional sexual abuse) than that being targeted by Robyn Stent, the principles are the same.

Schoener has since expanded on his remark in a personal communication with particular reference to churches, but again the applications are wider:

The purposes of discipline are:

a. to educate about a standard or a rule;

b. to inform people about its importance;

c. to deter others from doing the behaviour

d. to restore faith in the institution which is doing the discipline; and

e. for justice.

Each and every one of these purposes requires publication of discipline. In fact without publication, trust in the institution is undermined. (his emphasis)

One cannot expect people to come forward with complaints unless discipline is public and clearly visible. This is one way the church can distance itself from the abuse and appear credible. Many a church has hidden discipline and lost the confidence of its members in the process.

To this admirably clear analysis, I would add that the publication of discipline, once a complaint has been investigated and upheld, is a way for an institution, be it medical or ecclesiastical, to stand with the complainant in a public way, which can be a useful part of the healing process. It also facilitates approaches by any further complainants, who would be encouraged to think that what they have to say will be taken seriously and dealt with appropriately.

Here is an analogy for the responsibilities of institutions dealing with complaints towards the consumers of their spiritual, medical and other services, and to the wider community. It is like the health protection mechanism that swings into play if there is an outbreak of, say, hepatitis among customers of a food-outlet. Not only does the response include closure of the premises,a clean-out, safety inspections, not only does a carrier have to stay home and take his/her medication, but there is also widespread publicity to inform the community that there has been a risk to purchasers, potential symptoms are made known, and invitations to come forward for treatment are issued. And all this when the cause of the problem, the carrier, has been presumably unaware of the physical danger to others that they posed! Why shy away, then, from measures of this thoroughness when there have been culpable and toxic breaches of ethics by professionals into whose hands people have literally put their bodies and souls?

Some New Zealand churches are currently wrestling productively with this issue. Bishop Penny Jamieson did actually have a minister's name published in 1994 for offending – a courageous move! (*The Evening Post*, 16 November 1994) But the Methodist Church has declined requests from complainants to make public its disciplinary decisions in a case where there were multiple victims. These requests were made for the sorts of reasons outlined by Schoener, and by Stent's 'to promote and protect consumer rights.'

The Methodists, other churches, and apparently the Medical Council could take a leaf from the book of the Nursing Council. Even if the Council's processes are not sufficiently open for the Commissioner, nevertheless when it is in the public interest and/or an offence is serious, it does publish names and outcomes of disciplinary processes in the New Zealand Nurses' Organisation magazine, *Kai Tiaki Nursing New Zealand*. An example to be emulated by other institutions!

Where there is reluctance in the churches to do likewise, is fear of litigation by the minister an inhibiting factor? Is that all that keeps them silent? Or is corporate self-serving and protection of their own professional colleagues at the heart of these decisions? The question 'who gains?' must be asked whenever there are discussions where analysis of power is part of the equation. Will it be those who already have power? Is their power reinforced by a continuing silence? Or by the extraordinary logic of 'We're not keeping it secret, we're just not telling anyone'? Or could they move firmly to take the side of those who have already suffered because of misdemeanors of professionals? And of those whose well-being is put at risk when they determine that this knowledge shall not be made available to consumers?

A hard theological look at prioritising is necessary. Do the churches really believe in a God who is firmly on the side of the marginalised? The 'preferential option for the poor'? If they do, then that understanding must be applied here. Where there is a conflict of interests, whose interest is put ahead of who else's? I would suggest that to achieve justice the interests of various parties need to be consciously ordered: first – those of the victims; second – those of any potential victims, that is, congregations and others in contact with a known (to the church) abuser; third – the well-being and credibility of the church; and, only after all that, the interests of the perpetrator.

In the end, honest, humble responsibility-taking by institutions offers the best possibility of gain by all parties. Publication of names of offenders can redress the balance of power in favour of those who were harmed and disempowered by actions of professionals they had every reason to trust. It offers the wider community the protection of being able to make informed choices about whom to approach for care, be it spiritual or medical. It offers institutions an opportunity to restore damaged credibility and face the future with integrity. And diminishes the danger of litigation in the event of re-offending by an offender whose 'confidentiality' has been protected. It offers those who caused the problems the opportunity to take personal responsibility and grow through the experience, both personally and professionally.

The move to accountability to the community has seen the establishment of the Human Rights Commission, the Race Relations Conciliator's and the Health and Disability Commissioner's roles, and ombudsmen for the insurance and banking industries and the State Sector. If only there were a similar mechanism to which people could appeal about church processes experienced as inadequate or abusive, in efforts to 'promote and protect consumer rights'!

Visitors

Being in the
moment!

Last week my lawn did not get mown
Spring dandelions grew
To yellow toothed suns
And gentle globes
For puffing
These drew a charm of goldfinches
Who came with cherry faces
And yellow-barred wings
To visit

They lifted minute feet
To bend the hollow stems
And bring within reach
The treasure-trove of white-winged seeds
Jewelled creatures at a banquet
Honouring me with their presence
Feasting on the fruit of idleness
I'm glad my lawn did not get mown
Last week!

A Clergy Wife Speaks Out

It's over twenty years now since my minister-husband told me, when our third baby was nine weeks old, he thought I was mature enough to handle the news that he was having a liaison with a woman. I'd had my suspicions for over two years that something was amiss with the 'pastoral care' he'd been giving her, but had kept pretty quiet about it.

I was shattered, but could not face going to the church either for help or to complain. There were just too many fears. I would have seen myself as 'dobbing him in' – and I was sure others would have too. I would be creating division in my own family. Blame would be piled on me for not being a devoted and supportive wife. If I did go to the church and they took it seriously, it could lead to loss of our livelihood – unemployment for my husband if he were dismissed, and the consequent banishment from our church-owned home. The thought of wearing that kind of stigma was more than I could bear. Another probable scenario was that I would be exhorted 'to forgive and forget' and 'to turn the other cheek.' I'd already tried so hard to do that, but it was impossible: the horror, anger and sense of betrayal kept coming back to haunt me. If the hierarchy took action against him, I could come out of it worse than anyone.

A courageous woman, whom I'd met at the Melbourne Conference, asked me to write this article from her notes and to publish it on her behalf. It appeared in *Crosslink*, the Presbyterian/Methodist paper.

These are the reasons I kept quiet, at huge cost to myself; and why I suspect many other clergy wives do too when they discover that their husbands are perpetrators of sexual abuse. There's the love for your husband and family, social pressures to stay and endure, the threat of loss of community and lifestyle, and when there are young children it seems financially impossible. A loyalty trap, if ever there was one!

In desperation I eventually went to see his supervisor, another minister. He persuaded me that adultery is an adult activity, and no big deal. He gave me counselling about the marriage over six months while 'grooming' me, then sexualised the counselling relationship. During this time there was collusion between him and my husband – and I was declared to be suffering from paranoia, to be the one with the problems!

This, not surprisingly, caused me major difficulties: severe loss of confidence in my own judgement and high anxiety levels both affected my ability to parent, and wrecked my employment situation several times over. Eventually my husband was dismissed by the church for having another 'affair,' this time with another minister's wife. I coped by assenting to an 'open marriage,' and we left the church. I switched off emotionally and tried to rebuild some sort of separate existence. He eventually declared I didn't care enough, and left our marriage with yet another woman whom he'd been grooming for two years.

It took many years for me to recover and develop a professional life. Eventually I reconnected with the church and subsequently re-married. It was only about five years ago that I recognised and named what the minister/counsellor did to me as sexual abuse and abuse of power. He had manipulated me into complying with his own and my husband's sexually abusive behaviour. That minister has since died, and I have recently had an apology about all this from his organisation.

Reading *When Ministers Sin: Sexual Abuse in the Church* by Neil and Thea Ormerod provided me with a significant milestone. As a consequence I have done a complete turn-around in my attitude to my ex-husband's 'affairs.' I now believe that these women too, like myself, are his victims, even the one he married. I no longer view any of them as 'the other woman.'

By speaking out in this way, I want to raise awareness in the churches of the trauma suffered by women married to sexually abusive clergymen. Churches have begun dealing more usefully with the victims/survivors of sexual abuse by clergy. But I have not seen or heard of any appropriate pastoral care and support being given to wives and families of perpetrators. Our lives too have been devastated by the sexual abuse. How can the churches help us? One possibility is for support groups for such clergy wives to be facilitated. Another is skilled pastoral care to be offered while we are working our way back to emotional and spiritual health, care that understands and hopefully alleviates the pressures I have outlined. We also may need to be helped to leave the marriage – or the church – or both, to enable our healing.

(Name withheld)

The Violent Church

The institutional church, not surprisingly, has a very positive self-image. It is the Body of Christ, the House of God, the Barque of Peter – a safe haven, a source of healing and growth, the Way, a Community of Believers, a Pilgrim People. We like to invite others to be part of this institution because of the genuinely-held belief that it will do them good. Here, salvation – in the many ways that this can be understood – is available to all who enter in.

Sometimes the awareness of things that are individually distressing but true cannot be suppressed any longer. They need to be collected together and the pattern acknowledged.

In the terms of C G Jung, wholeness and maturity are only to be found through the sometimes terrifying process of facing up to one's shadow, one's dark side, being able to acknowledge it and then integrate it into one's self-understanding. It then becomes a treasure and an enriching resource for a more authentic existence. For there to be a more mature church in the new millennium, the church itself needs to undertake this painful voyage of discovery. There needs to be a holistic, courageous exploration of the injustices and violence perpetrated by the institutional church across its entire two thousand years of history, and a deep and full repentance, with a firm purpose of amendment.

There have been signs of examination of conscience, and a few rather inadequate piecemeal apologies – to women and to Jews; and of course Galileo and Teilhard de Chardin have been rehabilitated. But the violence hasn't stopped. Discussing the ordination of women is now an excommunicable transgression, and Matthew Fox, Leonardo Boff and Anthony de Mello who have together nourished millions are in the sin-bin.

The traditional rationalisation for the hurts suffered by people in the church context is 'oh well, it is a church of sinners.' Anywhere there are imperfect individuals, others will get inevitably get hurt; but the institution still sees itself as blameless and on track. This is no longer an acceptable response. While structural sin is a relatively new concept, human pain caused by those with ecclesiastical authority is not. So, yes, looking with 21st century judgements at the wrongs of the past may not be altogether fair. But on the other hand, if there is to be a move forward into a church that more truly represents the face of a just and compassionate God, such self-scrutiny and structural analysis are imperative.

If we look at the sweep of history there have been some consistent patterns of violence by the institutional church. Women, Jews, dissenters, homosexuals, scientists, indigenous peoples, and undoubtedly others, have been persecuted, have suffered and died in many ways at the hands of the institutional church.

Women's ministry was suppressed in the very early days of Christianity; they were abused in the writings of various church fathers; the first record of sexual abuse by clergy is from the fourth century; the first torture for witchcraft in the tenth century. Papal decree and the Dominican Fathers Kraemer and Springer unleashed three centuries of witch burnings on the world in which millions of women died; and official teachings now on women's issues do not take into account women's own perception of what is necessary and appropriate for their own well-being.

The church invented anti-semitism. Since the fourth century, when Jews were officially labelled as Christ-killers, they have been persecuted by Christians. This and later church persecutions gave rise to and sanctioned those by society at large. It is possible now to see the Crusades as naked aggression. And in the 14th century, Jews in the Papal States were required to wear yellow discs – Hitler was simply reviving an old Catholic practice! The official church scapegoating was readily adopted across society in a way that has enabled the church to say – 'but that wasn't us.' Attempts at official apologies have left many Jews saddened and unsatisfied. The big, long picture must be addressed, not just the window on the church involvement with the Holocaust.

A Sister Maria Renata Sanger was tortured for alleged lesbian activity in the 16th century. Frs John McNeil SJ and Felix Donnelly and no doubt others have been expelled from the priesthood in recent times for wanting a compassionate recognition of the lived reality of homosexuals. A recent Papal statement assured homosexuals that their very being was 'a state of objective disorder.' How does that help or heal?

The first official killings of dissenters by the church of the gospel were in the seventh century, during the Donatist heresy. They gathered momentum through to the Inquisition of the 14th and 15th centuries, and the killing of Catholics and dissenters by each other in Tudor England. Theologians who have fallen into disfavour were mentioned earlier. And in the 1990s, a loyalty declaration is required of those who teach theology in Catholic institutions.

Henry II of England was in 1155 authorised by the Pope to subdue Ireland. The bloody consequences of that move have only recently begun to be constructively addressed. Later, missionaries participated in the conquering and colonising of millions of indigenous people from the discovery of the New World in 1492 through to the 20th century. The spiritualities of indigenous peoples, the expression of their very souls, were taken from them along with land and language. Even now it is not rare to hear Māori spirituality described as 'demonic.' While this is not an official position it comes from the original missionary attitude that 'outside the church there is no salvation.'

So, as well as great good and great hope, the church of Christ has unleashed upon the world great violence and great harm to millions over its twenty centuries. This is a good time for an owning of the shadow, for a confession of sin – not of the 'bless me Father, I stole an apple' type, but the mature confession that is ready to acknowledge responsibility for and repercussions from violent official church decisions and policies. Only then will credibility be restored, and a forgiving world perhaps be willing and able to access the treasures that are truly available through Christ's church.

Scripture tells us that God is to be found among the marginal people. A preferential option for the poor is enshrined in Catholic social teaching. These people then – women, Jews, homosexuals, indigenous people and dissenters – are the poor, the anawim,[21] and are so because of direct church policies and actions. These are the ones the institutional church must look to with humility and respect. They hold the key to the rediscovery and revitalising of its God-given task of bringing hope and healing to the world of the next millennium.

As Jung said, the gold is in the shadow, and entering willingly into the shadow generates new life!

Consenting Adults or Organisational Incest?

In the maelstrom of verbiage on the Clinton-Lewinsky affair there are two concepts which I have yet to see named – 'organisational incest' and 'abuse of power.' To do this is to invite a very different perspective from that couched in words of 'It's his private life,' 'everyone makes mistakes,' 'let him get on with being President,' etc. It is to doubt the ability of a powerful man to exercise power appropriately in his immediate environment; and if he is not capable of this in the micro world of his personal relationships, how can he be deemed capable of doing so in the macro world of national politics and international relationships?

Once one has learned about power dynamics, patriarchal misuse of power becomes evident in all sorts of settings. This was an opinion piece published in *The Evening Post*. It was apparently discussed over many workplace morning teas.

Let us look first at the issue of consent: much has been written in recent times about the impossibility of validation of consent where there is a significant power imbalance. This is why there are ethical guidelines outlawing sexualised behaviour/relationships by counsellors, doctors, clergy etc. Peter Rutter's book, *Sex in the Forbidden Zone*, extends this framework to include employment and mentoring relationships. He describes with brutal honesty the ambivalence that hearing revelations of such behaviours can arouse: some recognition of their wrongness, but at the same time a wish to do likewise, and therefore an unwillingness to condemn. Women *can* find powerful men attractive, and fifty-something year old men *can* wish to reconnect with their lost youth with a younger woman. That much is common humanity.

But with power comes responsibility. Let us look at Clinton: male, mature (in years at least), rich, married to a loyal wife, holder of the most powerful job in the world, the employer. Then at Monica Lewinsky: female, nineteen years old, his employee in possibly her first job. In every way he had significantly more power, and therefore, it must be understood, more responsibility. His task in relation to her was to act in her best interests and refrain from using his position to manipulate and sexually abuse, because that is how what occurred must be named. And to take the next step, it must be named, in the phrase coined by American psychologist William White as long ago as the 1970s, 'organisational incest.'

Incest in the family context is rightfully a crime. It is known to have devastating effects on the child concerned for an indefinite number of years. No area of life is unaffected – the emotional, the social, the economic, the spiritual. It is characterised by secrecy. The injunction 'don't tell' is invariably reinforced with threats, and 'if you do, no-one will believe you anyway.' Breaking the silence is a fearful thing to contemplate. Dad might go to jail. Mum has difficulty believing the story as it threatens her family structure and whole world. She may at some level blame the child for the repercussions, adding to the pain the child already feels.

In the organisational arena, recognition is much, much slower that similar types of damage are done to less powerful adults, usually women, by employers like Bill Clinton, and other professionals who engage them in sexual behaviour. There is a power inherent in hierarchical structures that replicates that of families. This enables similar abuses – and similar dynamics occur when these revelations are made: the denials, the minimising, the blaming the victim, the diversionary tactics. Over the last few months we have heard them all! The language of 'boundaries' and 'appropriate behaviour' has barely begun to become common currency.

The President has a 'paternal' position in the White House organisational family. Lewinsky is young enough to be his daughter. Her well-being, and that of all his staff members, ought to have taken precedence over his self-gratification, as in any healthy family, organisational or otherwise.

Much attention has been paid to how the 'Lewinsky affair' has damaged Clinton and his position. The question must also be asked: how has the 'Clinton affair' damaged Monica Lewinsky and her future? How would you rate her chances now of having a healthy, fulfilling relationship within the next ten years? Or getting a job which will enable her to fulfil her potential? Or of being treated with the respect she is entitled to as a young woman starting out in life? It seems she has barely begun to grieve for the relationship she thought she had with him, and which he has now effectively disowned. It may take her a while yet to realise she has been a victim of abuse of power of a most reprehensible kind.

In terms of consent, what chance did she realistically have of saying 'no'? Who says 'no' to the President about anything? It most emphatically was not a case of two consenting adults! Kathleen Willey, even with the advantage of more years, still experienced the same power dynamic: 'You can't slap the President of the United States!'

And a man who can indulge in such gross abuse of power must endure questioning of his trustworthiness and integrity. It is *not* simply a private peccadillo, to be glossed over as quickly as possible. It *does* have a bearing on his fitness for office. Consenting adults? No way! Let's use the accurate description of the whole mess: it was organisational incest and abuse of power.

Millennium

We'd thought of them as slightly mad
The ones who thought He'd come again in glory
As the clock ticked midnight
(Just whose midnight was never clear!)

We, the more rational Christians, knew better
But to my surprise
I have seen my Christ on earth this week gone by

I have seen Him in the work and planning
Of communities large and small
Down and across Aotearoa
Right around the globe –
Ordinary people joining together
To make and mark the celebratory Moments
To karanga the New Day

I have seen Him in the glories
Of humanly created star-bursts
Flying ferns and fizzing fires
Our puny imitations of the Big Bang
Joy to child-hearts watching round the world
Wellington, Sydney, Paris, London and New York
As our orb rolled to the magic instant of clock-time
And through to the new realm of numbers

I have seen Him in the awe of billions
As with bated breaths we watched –
Really watched – the miracle
Of sun sinking below horizon
Swathed in green and gold
To swing under the belly of our night
We watched it rise in glory from mists of other seas
A daily miracle, usually largely ignored
Yet on that Day we humans
Again turned our faces towards the cosmos
And worshipped with bull-roarer and conch horn

Watching television coverage of the countdown to the end of the 20th century and the beginning of the 21st brought many perceptible Christ-moments.

I have seen Him in the hopeful hearts
The cries for times of peace and truth
And food enough for all
The wish for new beginnings
The turning over of new leaves
The honouring of our old people
As gifts from the past
And of our children
As torch-bearers to the future
A new world dawning

I have seen Him in the gathering of the threads
The looking back, the reminiscences
The discernings of patterns, trends and greatness
In the life of the earth and its peoples
The sense of being with and for each other
Of one human family
Of being part of making history
At the dawn of the third Millennium
Since His birth

Yes, He has come again!
Could we but keep alive this new awareness
Of life, creation and each other!
Jesus, stay with us! Please!

Unless You Become as Little Children…

God-moments in the ordinary – living more deeply into the meaning of Scripture truths…

I'm a late starter as far as tramping is concerned. The bush has always had a strong attraction, but I didn't ever think my fitness level was up to tramping club standards. So I jumped at the chance recently to go with three other fifty-somethings for a two-day trip in the Tararua ranges, north of Wellington. According to the literature, our first three hours' walk would be alongside a stream and 'easy.' And so it was. Except for the bit that I took one look at and decided was impossible.

Imagine a path about twenty centimetres wide, with a slight lean towards the edge, and over the edge a ten-metre drop to the river. To make matters worse the surface of the path had some loose shingle; and even worse again, the inner curve of the path was a high clay bank with nothing to hold on to. I've never liked edges. I knew I couldn't get round there even without a pack on – let alone with! Several options were apparent: I could go back alone; I could pretend it was no problem, swallow the fear and have a go, while knowing for sure I'd end up on the rocks below; I could simply refuse to try – or I could risk being real. One of my companions was a very old friend – we've known each other nearly forty years now. I could actually be honest with her about my fear. She had already bounded like a mountain goat across to other side. Why couldn't I do that? And the voices of doom inside shrieked louder and louder 'You'll fall! You'll fall!'

'I'm too scared,' I said. Her response was utterly accepting and without judgement. 'Would it help if I came back and held your hand?' 'Yes, please.' And she did. I took the outstretched hand and despite the cold sweat of terror actually made it to the other side, with a sense of being aged about four. Once there, along with the relief, some thing inside me was being re-made. I had actually – with support – accomplished a task that five minutes earlier had looked totally impossible. The little four-year old girl inside suddenly had a new sense of competence. This new taste of the abundant life that Jesus promises was exciting stuff!

It dawned on me that I had just lived Matthew 18:3. I had quite literally become as a little child, and the reward was indeed great. I had been enabled to enter the Promised Land in both literal and metaphorical terms. In choosing to drop the mask, the illusion of independent adulthood, the pride – and admit the reality of my fear, and in accepting the calm offer of help, I had discovered some more of my own potential.

Children in general do not hide their feelings – that is something we learn to do as we get older. Jesus talked about eternal life being now. So those moments when we can become as little children, reveal our fears, find them respected, get appropriate support and discover we can transcend our hitherto limits are truly heavenly moments.

We walked on through the bush. Fern fronds unfurled in celebration, trees clapped their hands, the river cheered and tūī belled alleluias. And I prayed a thanksgiving – for safety, for the grace to take the risks, and for my friend who had truly been the Christ-bearer, holding out her hand to me in my paralysis of fear.

The next day we retraced our steps, as weather conditions made our proposed route unwise. That three metres of narrow path was still scary – but no longer impossible. If I'd managed it once, I could do it again. The help was again offered, and again accepted with relief and gratitude. Becoming the child was easier this time. We made it! Another God-moment to savour. Another taste of heaven.

The Emperor's New Clothes

I write to encourage Fr Pat Maloney and any other pastors who have been brave enough to think as he has thought and written in the article 'How Merciful is the Catholic Church?' (*Tui Motu InterIslands*, September 2000).

It has long been a puzzle to me that many priests can and do offer quality, appropriate care to people coming for pastoral guidance, be they trying to escape an abusive marriage, contemplating a second one, pondering contraception, or identifying as gay or lesbian. The puzzle is that the appropriate, supportive care is frequently at variance with the official teaching of the church as proclaimed and preached. As an interested lay person I have applauded the choices made by such priests, but wonder what sort of tension is created for them. How must it be for priests to live astride this split between the public teaching and the private pastoral care that can be so radically different?

Occasionally a brave priest will venture to question the advisability of official church teachings. To be encouraged – because it is ultimately their voices, rather than those of dissident lay women, which are likely to move the institution towards asking 'what would Jesus do?' and then doing likewise.

There are several aspects to this, which seem important. One is the reality that people are more likely to be able to make better moral choices if they meet with a loving acceptance, than if they are presented with a rule book and instructions to measure up or be cast out. Can you think of a time in your life when this proved to be the case? Which attitude has been the more genuinely useful and enabling? The answer to this question is surely the same as to the question 'what would Jesus do?' Loving acceptance is the way of Jesus and, as Father Maloney said, he did have a preference for the companionship of what might be called the 'B team' of the human race.

Father Maloney suggests that a more merciful church would actually be more useful for both the people and the institution (for credibility and retention are indeed problems). This approach still seems to me to be somewhat demeaning to the people involved – they could be 'let off,' have their 'weaknesses' taken into account, knowing that 'the Lord still loves them.' They can be 'permitted' to give God a second-rate offering. But I prefer to think of a God who positively wants the life-giving options for people with difficult issues.

My contribution to this discussion is the suggestion that good pastoral guidance is actually based on an alternative sound and workable theology, rather than somehow just side-stepping the 'givens.' I believe such compassionate pastoral care is based on an Exodus theology. What liberates you? What is life-giving for you? How is God's invitation to you visible in the options you see? God did not encourage the Hebrews to stay in their bondage, to turn the other cheek, to forgive. What they were offered was the journey to freedom, long and desperate as it was. But at the end was the promise of a better life. Jesus promised 'life, and life to the full,' and that the blind would see, the lame would walk and the captives would be set free. Is not compassionate pastoral guidance a fulfilment of that promise? So to Father Maloney and pastors of similar persuasion I would say: 'Take heart. You are on the right track, the Way of Jesus. You have been asking yourselves "what would Jesus do?" and finding the answer of acceptance and compassion.'

Nonetheless, this all highlights another credibility problem. To have official teaching and pastoral practice at variance with each other causes problems. Because if people of faith who are struggling with these issues, desperately trying to 'keep the rules,' only know of the existence of the public teaching, they are being wilfully kept in darkness. They are being hampered in their search for God's way to live their particular lives. Keeping public silence about compassionate pastoral solutions, effectively keeping them secret, is colluding with oppression.

Once upon a time if you wanted to know the 'will of God,' you looked to the church for a description thereof. This came packaged in the absolutes, in the theologies that are seriously flawed because they ignore the key consideration of the lived experiences of those most intimately concerned. Now people are looking more to experience a God who makes sense humanly, because what is human good sense is not separate from spiritual good sense; in the words of psychologist Jack Dominian, 'a God who makes us feel lovable.' (*Tui Motu InterIslands*, December 1998) No longer is it healthy to have an authoritarian, patriarchal God who tosses down the rule book and then watches us flounder and agonise as we attempt to measure up.

How much more life-giving to have a God who wants what is good for us, whatever that may entail! Jesus cursed the Pharisees for adding to the burdens of the people. A church which adds to burdens rather than relieving them is not in the mould of the Christ. So, 'yes' to mercy, but an even louder 'yes' to recognising the Christ Way as authentically present in gentle, accepting support for people's lived realities as they engage in wrestling with moral choices.

Reflections on a Transition

Moving house in recent weeks for only the third time in the almost forty years since my marriage has begun a new phase of my life. It's a time to review the journey, check the maps. Statistically speaking, given my rapid approach to sixty, this is where the final quarter of my life could well be spent.

'Transition' was the designated topic for an issue of *Vashti's Voices*. A good moment for reflection on those currently taking place in my own life.

At the moment it's like a honeymoon – I'm besotted with the house, the view of air, land and water (Wellington Harbour, the airport, the Orongorongos, Pencarrow, Baring Head, Cook Strait), by the capaciousness of cupboards slanting back under the sloping roof, the exposed beams and skylights, the tiny but well-endowed garden, the twelve hours of uninterrupted sun. I have a developing relationship with the previous owner who lived here for nearly twenty years and died here in June. She was a musician, a former member of the New Zealand Symphony Orchestra, and had a grand piano in the lounge and a smaller one in the room where she gave lessons. She was apparently a gutsy and humorous woman. The house is echoing with her music and I won't be surprised when I hear drifts of Chopin or Liszt floating upstairs some still midnight.

The external precipitating factor for the move was the departure of the last of my seven children to go flatting. I waited a decent six months to see whether he wanted to come home again, but it didn't happen. There would be room for him here if necessary. But mowing a large lawn on which no-one any longer kicked balls around, rattling with empty bedrooms and far more space than I needed, seemed a bit pointless.

So I began the hunt for a new home – and found a pretty good match for my long list of requirements. It's the first time I have had a home of my very own, and it's like being seven again and playing house. I went from the parental home at twenty to the house my husband already owned. We up-sized twelve years later after the arrival of four children and a commitment to a foster daughter. Twenty years and two more babies later, well into an early widowhood, and with only those two youngest still at home, I downsized. And now, six years since then, I'm here!

I've literally moved from a valley, somewhat dark and chilly in winter, up into the sun, up to where I can see a long way, to where the Southern Cross hangs on its head outside my bedroom window just before dawn streaks apricot across the mountains. And this shift reflects the inner journey to a treasured and inviting crone-hood. If I'm knocked over by a bus tomorrow I'm well aware that a cub reporter would describe me as 'an elderly woman.' But I've never felt younger or happier – or been fitter either, for that matter. Our large family, the culture of the times and sundry other influences have meant that despite university degrees and an assortment of other training a full-time career has eluded me. Frustrating at times, but the up-side of this is ample time to nurture myself, my friendships, to respect my own needs and rhythms, to think my own thoughts, choose my own path in ways that seemed – and were – totally unthinkable at any other stage of my life. Financially, a widow's benefit and odds and ends of work encourage the Quaker value of simplicity, and a frugality which is still comfortable enough.

During the hard times the Voice that kept promising 'I will make up to you for the years that the locusts have eaten' often seemed like an extra burden. But now seems like the fulfilment of the promise. There is safety, security, the richness of friendships, the occasional reverence for my white hair (tarnished now and then by young men who call me 'Dear'). 'Becoming as a little child' has its importance – like the one in the story of the Emperor's New Clothes. These days I say what I see, no longer worried that if no-one else says they see it too that it isn't there. There is nothing at stake, nothing that can be taken away from me. That is the privilege of marginalisation, of unemployment.

The offspring are now, all seven of them, a source of satisfaction as they get on with their lives in, by and large, constructive and competent ways. My five grandchildren are a delight, and I look forward to their coming to love this new house too. So many places for hide-and-seek, their special cupboard with toys and puzzles, the plastic globe of the jaffa dispenser, and a grandmother who looks forward to watching them grow up and giving them a serene place to visit as they develop in an ever more complex and accelerating world.

It would be great to live healthily and happily for another twenty-five years – and with parents who are still doing that at 85, genetically speaking there's a reasonable chance I could. I do not yet know what it feels like to lose a parent. I passionately want all my friends to last as long as I do. But death among my peers is no longer the aberration, the outrage that it was when we were thirty. It is sadly becoming more 'normal.' Not that we get to choose, but for myself I would like enough notice of my own impending death to be able to orchestrate the conclusions that feel necessary. Having worked briefly at Mary Potter Hospice, I can't think of a safer place to be for that final life-experience. Should I be given that notice next week I'd be mildly frustrated, but it would be okay. I think!

Formally leaving the church in which I had spent my entire life has been truly liberating. The crumbling relationship was as painful as a divorce must be. But no longer feeling embarrassed by and guiltily complicit in the un-Christ-like doings of the institution is just fine. The ExAlt community and Sophia (Catholic feminist network) are 'church' for me – and God (who long since had to stop being a He) is the Presence, the Energy, the Source, the Now, the Destination, the Love that passes vibrantly between me and others, the One who permeates my living alone with a peaceful bubbling-up of joy from the deep well.

So this is a good place to be! The years of stress and pain and frantic slogging hard work, running all day just to stay in the same place, are over. I'm learning to sing again, re-discovering a long-buried sense of humour, waking up purring every morning and going to bed the same way. What more could I ask!

Potential

I have a dream
A dream for the Christian church
A dream of a way it could celebrate the
2000th anniversary,

> give or take, of the birth of the Jesus
> whose life and mission it sees itself as embodying.

The church preaches truth, compassion and justice.
It sees itself as a beacon of light in a world of darkness,
As sanctuary, salvation,
safety to those who take refuge in it.
But the experience of many, many people is of being hurt and harmed

> by those whose task it was to help.

A Millennium reflection, born from my frustration and that of many others in trying to get basic justice from churches.

My dream is this: that the scales fall from the eyes of the institutional churches

> that they look with new clarity at their own internal workings
> and honestly compare what they see with what they proclaim.

I would like them to understand

> that far from being leaders in the ways of truth, compassion and justice,
> they actually are lagging behind secular society
> in some very important areas.

If the scales fell from their eyes

> how then could the churches justify their exemption from
> Human Rights legislation?
> how then could they continue with sexist and homophobic theologies?
> how then could authoritarian injustices be perpetrated and defended?
> how then could structures that depend on lack of accountability be sustained?

I dream that the scales will fall from their eyes

> and they will recapture the vision of a church culture
> that practises what it preaches,
> a church that walks the talk.

The losses could be great, but the gains would be immeasurable.
Credibility and authenticity are such precious and attractive attributes.

I doubt that my dream will come true next month, next year, or even next century.

But in the meantime I have an idea.
We have ombudsmen for the state sector,
the banking and insurance industries.
There are Commissioners for Human Rights, Children, Race Relations, Health and
Disability.
These roles all establish accountability to the wider community,

> the right of appeal when someone is not satisfied
> with the way they have been dealt with.

What I'd like to see is an ombudsman for church affairs – an impartial person entrusted

> with examining the justice of church dealings with individuals and groups.

At the moment if one disagrees with a church decision,

> there is no place to go – nowhere that is, but out the door.

Such an ombudsman, jointly funded by all the churches,

> would be a pledge to the wider community of the intention
> of the churches
> to deal fairly, honestly and transparently with everyone
> both internally and externally.

It would be a sign of a commitment to Shalom,
to a peace based on God's justice.
To give birth to such a concept would be a
fitting celebration of the new millennium.
I dream of a labour leading towards this birth,
I dream of the birth of a healthier church however it may come.

Fierce Feathers   *2001*

'The shortest distance between truth and the human
heart is a story.'

Anthony de Mello

A moment
of drama at a
Quaker Meeting
for Worship.

Have you ever been peacefully minding your own business then
suddenly discovered that you are a participant in a drama? This
happened to me and all the other people at meeting for worship at Wellington Meeting
on the third Sunday in March. This is the Sunday of the month when the children spend
time in hearing stories and doing related activities before joining us for the last fifteen
minutes of the meeting. The door opens and they sidle in with a few whisperings and
scufflings, and sit on the little seats strategically placed between larger ones. Sometimes
they tell us what they have been doing. We smile lovingly, and appreciate the work and
creativity the mums, dads and others have used to teach the young ones their heritage.

But on this particular Sunday, the doors swung open and nothing happened. All was still
and silent. I just had to look and so I'm sure did everyone else. There were half a dozen
or more Indian braves of assorted sizes standing in the doorway, complete with war-paint
and feather head-dresses – and tomahawks too! What the …?!! My first thought was that
this was all rather incongruous given the Quaker context. Still the silence and stillness
as we looked at them and they looked at us. And then the penny dropped. We were all
re-enacting the story of Fierce Feathers. Suddenly we were audience no longer but all
of us players in the drama that was unfolding. And yes, having looked at their fill and
recognised their Great Spirit at work, the Indians all quietly filed to the empty seats, laid
down their weapons and entered into the silence. Among the adults, a joyous recognition.
It was a most enchantingly holy moment!

We sat in Spirit-filled silence together, and when the meeting was closed, one of the
mums explained what the children had been learning, and some of the young Indians
moved quietly around the room giving us each a white feather of peace. The story of
how angry Indians came to the meeting house of Easton Township, Saratoga County,
New York, in the summer of 1775, to kill the only whites left in the area, stayed to
share silence, then left as friends, has been the subject of several paintings. In this year of
2001 we did not need the same courage to trust for our physical safety that the original
participants had shown. The self-control back then was truly awesome, as men, women
and children continued sitting quietly doing what they had come to do, and wordlessly

conveying an offer of friendship. The spirits of the Indians had been met with peace and they were moved to respond the same way.

I was deeply moved by this surprise of finding myself a participant in a story of 'back then,' which was not just being re-enacted but truly re-experienced in the present. It reminded me of the Jewish understanding of Passover, of anamnesis, of 'remembering by being in.' The power of the foundational event continues flowing like a river and every remembering is not separate and disconnected, but a new immersion into the present, potent actuality of the old story.

So this story without words took us back two hundred and twenty-six years, held us in the present moment, then took us forward in our own lives with an invitation to live more deeply in the Spirit of Peace.

Proclaiming Liberty to Captives…

Celebrating Paulo Freire, whose educational philosophies provide a framework for Women's Refuge, Liberation Theology, and other movements working for human dignity.

All people are called to act upon the world, moving towards a fuller, richer life both as individuals and collectively. This is the basic assumption of Brazilian educator, Paulo Freire. He was born in 1921 and had his own experience of extreme poverty as a child. Later he drew on the works of many philosophers to wrestle with the questions 'why is it like this?' and 'why does it continue to be like this?' and 'is there anything I can do about it?' He eventually became Professor of the History of the Philosophy of Education at Recife University, Brazil.

In the 1960s he was invited to develop a literacy programme for his country, where 93 percent of the population were illiterate. His first moves were to listen and to look. He and his team went to where the people were. They listened to the conversation topics of men and women in the town squares, the barbershops, at weddings and funerals. They noted the themes that recurred – lack of health care, inadequate housing, the pricing of seeds, the injustice of landlords. They noted the ignorance and lethargy, the great silence of the dispossessed, and saw that this was the direct product of the social and political domination of which these people were victims. Critical awareness and response to oppression were virtually impossible for them. He also concluded that any education system either challenges or actively maintains the status quo.

So from that basis he designed the literacy programme. The reading and writing were taught: the subject matter was the themes that concerned the peasants. Within a month they were often able to read. But more than that: they were being given the tools to look at their own reality, to observe the bigger picture. With this came a new awareness of self, a sense of dignity and new hope. Freire called this Critical Awareness. They discovered their own potency, and were no longer willing to be the simply the objects of domination by the rich and powerful. They became able to challenge the ancient historical belief that the oppression of groups within hierarchies is 'natural' or 'common sense,' or 'God's way.'

They learnt to perceive political and economic contradictions and to take action individually and collectively against oppressive groups and individuals. It is a known fact that oppression is rarely if ever self-limiting. Oppressors have too much to gain from being in power to recognise any need for change. Only when the oppressed talk together, then stand together to say 'that's enough,' is there the ghost of a chance for change. Freire's literacy programme was dramatically successful – but it threatened the establishment, and so he found himself in prison for several months for endangering the state. Tyrants always have an interpretation of reality that protects their self-interest, and the description of tyranny from their victims' point of view threatens destabilisation of their world.

He describes his methodology and principles in his books, notably in *Pedagogy of the Oppressed*. These are used in a variety of settings worldwide to help oppressed people come to an understanding of their situation and to gain the strength to challenge it.

One of these settings was a house in Newtown, Wellington, where a few years ago I was co-facilitating a 10-week course for women who were or had been victims of domestic violence. They were provided with a safe environment in which they could – often for the first time – name and describe the realities of their lives. The lethargy and the great silence of the dispossessed that Freire noted were initially seen there, too. They were invited to break this silence. 'What has it been like?' the coordinator asked. They told her and each other. They were invited to dream: How would you like your life to be different? Freire's questions are posed: Why did it happen? Why does it continue? What can I do to stop it? Social analysis such as the power wheel was offered, and discussion invited on what they recognised as applicable to themselves.

Regrettably, tyranny is still alive and well in many homes in Aotearoa New Zealand. It is not just the prerogative of third-world despots. The women were encouraged to have a wider perspective, to look at the personal, the cultural and the institutional elements of their predicaments; to see that their situations were instigated and/or compounded by cultural beliefs about men's and women's roles, and by institutional responses and teachings. In other words, to place their personal story into a wider context and to see it as part of a big picture.

And slowly hope dawned. Very slowly. Some women went through the course several times, getting something new from it each time. An integral part of Freire's method is that action follows reflection. So the question 'What can I or we do about this?' is crucially important. For some women simply responding to the suggestion to say 'no' to someone about something during the next week seemed a huge step. Sometimes it was writing a group letter to the newspaper on an issue they felt passionate about. Sometimes it was inviting someone from an institution to come and hear what they had to say. Gradually strength grew, and leaving a damaging relationship became a possibility. Often the precipitating factor was seeing the disastrous effects that living with violence had on their children.

Always this choice was of necessity left with the individual woman. She was encouraged to look at her fears, the obstacles, the resources needed, the possible consequences. Was it better to risk claiming freedom, or leave things to remain the same indefinitely? The risk was not insignificant – more women are killed or injured by partners when they have just broken out of a relationship than at any other time. Laying claim to the basic Human Rights of freedom from want, freedom from fear, freedom of thought and speech can be as personally risky in New Zealand as under a repressive political regime. Frequently the law fails to provide effective protection. Women who reach out in this way for a more human life for themselves and their children deserve a medal. It takes huge courage.

They, and the facilitators who worked with them, owe a debt of gratitude to Paulo Freire for his ground-breaking work as an educator/philosopher in creating the theory of critical thinking, and reflection-action, with its applications to claiming freedom. And a debt of gratitude is owed to the women of Duluth, Minnesota, who developed the power and equality wheels, for translating these into a form to help with this very specific form of tyranny.

What does all this have to do with us? If we are enduring any sort of tyranny in our own lives, perhaps we can use Paulo Freire's questions and tools of analysis to look at our situation. If we are not directly affected we can take to heart his words:

It is a historical fallacy that any group of people has the right to oppress any other group.

And

Washing one's hands of the conflict between the powerful and the powerless means to side with the powerful, not to be neutral.

The Christ-call is to stand in solidarity with victims as they learn to claim their right to be free.

Therapy

The roaring screaming
Yelling face
Caused the cowering
Way at the back
And to appease
The flinging out
Of tiny corpse
To be devoured
The life-light
Dimmed and paled
In the depths
Formless

My psychotherapy journey continued – with moments of awe and gratitude for the agape and commitment I was experiencing. And for the Divinely-designed process of the unconscious emerging to consciousness.

This time's different
Waiting peace
Leaves space enough
To let the sunlight in
Undemanding
Waiting
Silent waiting
No need to split and fling
Sweetness steals in
I can uncurl
Then in one piece
Tiptoe to the threshold
And stand in the sun
Intact

A Quaker Saint

A woman sat writing a letter by a window. Her name was Margaret Fell and the year was 1666. It was no ordinary window – it was the grille of a stone-walled prison cell in Lancaster Castle in the north of England. It was no ordinary letter – it was a letter to King Charles II to ask for her own freedom and that of the many hundreds of her Friends languishing in prison throughout the land.

She was no ordinary woman: intelligent, educated, articulate, strong-minded, a well-endowed land-owner, and deeply spiritual. By 1664, when she was first imprisoned at 52 years of age, she was the widow of a judge, a devoted mother of nine children of whom eight were surviving into adulthood, and one of the most dedicated followers of George Fox, the founder of Quakerism. She had already made four trips to London to plead personally with the King for religious tolerance for Quakers and other dissenters from the Established Church. She travelled the 400 kilometres to London ten times in all, on horse-back and later by coach, and the last of those occasions was when she was eighty-three. By then there was legislation that gave tolerance of freedom for worship. This improvement in the situation was in no small part due to her and George Fox. The Catholics of that time also benefitted.

But the 1660s were an era when it was considered treasonable to be anything other than an attending, tithe-paying, card-carrying member of the Church of England. Religion and politics were as horribly intertwined as they still are in some parts of the world. All she and the other Quakers wanted was the freedom to worship their God in peace, to hold Meetings for Worship, the silent waiting on God that is still the norm for Quakers. And they campaigned for this freedom from a position of non-violent resistance. They did not desert their principles on the grounds that the end justified the means.

Margaret Fell was imprisoned four times in Lancaster Castle, the last time when she was 69. That first imprisonment lasted for four years. Her 'crimes' were twofold: refusing to promise that she would no longer hold Meetings for Worship in her home, and refusing to take the Oath of Allegiance to the King. This latter stance was based on Quaker belief that there should not be two qualities of truth to be told. They take seriously Jesus' words in Matthew 5:34-37: 'Do not swear oaths … All you need to say is 'yes' if you mean yes, and 'no' if you mean no; anything more than this comes from the evil one.' From their position has eventually come the opportunity to choose to affirm in a court of law, rather than swear on the Bible. For these two 'crimes' Margaret was sentenced to life imprisonment and the forfeiture of all her property.

The physical conditions in her cell in the castle were grim. As she wrote to the King: 'It is so wet with rain and snow that in the winter-time it is not fit for neither beasts nor dogs

I visited Lancaster Castle as a child, but only much more recently 'met' one of its famous prisoners. The idea that the spiritual equality of women and men was argued from Scripture in 1666 fascinated me, as did its unquestioned acceptance ever since in the Quaker world.

to lie in.' It seems that there was some leniency shown to this special prisoner and the other Quakers imprisoned with her. They were sometimes allowed to meet together for worship – the very 'crime' they'd been imprisoned for! Margaret was allowed her family to visit, and on one occasion allowed a home visit. Most importantly she was allowed to have her Bible and writing materials. And in the four years before the King eventually relented and released her, she wrote four books. Contemporary commentators drew parallels between the King and the Pharaoh: did the devastating Plague in 1665 and the Great Fire of London in 1666 help him to hear her plea to 'let my people go'?

She was a prolific writer, eventually producing sixteen books on assorted topics, countless letters to her large family, to friends, and to various eminent people, and twenty-seven Epistles to Quaker groups around England. One book which is of particular pertinence to our times was written in Lancaster Castle: *Women's speaking justified, proved and allowed of by the Scriptures, all such as speak by the spirit and power of the Lord.* Over three hundred years ago she produced Scriptural arguments for the spiritual equality of men and women, which have been re-discovered in the last twenty years and are familiar to many women now. She wrote of the women prophets in the Hebrew Scriptures, Jesus' respect for women, their faithfulness to him even to the Cross, and their first knowledge of the Resurrection. And she used St Paul's own words to mitigate some of his apparently anti-woman statements. She pleaded with men not to try to limit the power of God by believing it exists only in their own sex. Spiritual equality between men and women has always been part of Quaker beliefs – George Fox himself wrote two books on the same topic.

Margaret married George Fox in 1669. They already had, and continued in, a deep spiritual union, but spent very little time together because of their various imprisonments and missionary journeys. He died in 1691 and she in 1702. They both had laboured to get a sound structure for the infant movement, and to get the principle of religious liberty enshrined in English law.

And still the principles they established for Quaker living remain: seeking guidance of the Inner Light, speaking the truth, the equality of all human beings, recognising 'that of God' in every person, simplicity, justice, non-violence, and active peace-making. With good reason is Margaret Fell known as the Mother of Quakerism.

Transformation

A change or alteration, especially a radical one; the act of transforming or the state of being transformed.

Another *Vashti's Voices* special topic article, written on request and just after 9/11.

As I write this, two weeks after the New York disaster, the world knows that history turned a sharp corner that day, both personally and politically. That act of terrorism brutally transformed our understanding of personal safety, national security, evil and goodness. It caused a chaos that even when this goes to print is unlikely to have been resolved. Maybe we are on the brink of World War III, or maybe President Bush's immature rhetoric and intentions will have gentled under the influence of wiser counsel from people who know that violence only ever breeds more. Why avenge the loss of 5000 lives by the choosing to sacrifice 10,000 more? Maybe he and others will have learned to listen, so that peace based on understanding and justice becomes more likely.

Before the cataclysm of that week, my ponderings about transformation had been around the small, the personal, the different ways these things take place. I remembered the spring ritual in my early childhood in England of bringing home frog-spawn from the canal in a jam-jar with a handle made of string, a slithery handful of jelly dots each with a tiny, black eye. This mass went into a fish-bowl with enough water-weed to make a home for the little eyes as they grew, developed tails and eventually jerked their way to freedom. Watching them fatten up took a long time. Then excitement! It started happening: tiny buds below the tail brought forth the first pair of legs, then the front ones appeared as the tail began to shrink, the contours of the head changed, and eyes began to bulge. To hold a tiny perfectly formed froglet was another of the miracles of childhood. They were then taken back to their natural habitat and watched with satisfaction as they demonstrated their ability to leap now, as well as swim.

And drops of rain. At six I could not imagine the grey splats sliding down the window to be truly the same substance that with the help of an emerging sun becomes a rainbow. Glorious, glowing and containing the essence of every colour in the universe, symbol of hope and promise, with stories trailing in its wake – like the arc I saw many years later from my bedroom window when I woke on the morning of my husband's funeral. There had never been one outside that window before and there never was again. Again in England, and still I am ignorant of the science involved, I marvelled at the rainbows captured in petrol leaks on rain-black roads, even as the rain still pelted down. My fantasy was that these were baby rainbows waiting to grow up enough to fly.

More wonders as my childhood was transplanted to New Zealand: what exactly happens inside a monarch chrysalis, itself a miracle of green with gold trimmings? Maybe a scientist somewhere has been able to watch via ultra-sound as the yellow, black and white striped caterpillar skin is shed and the small being inside it shelters in an apparently inert casing until any semblance to its previous form has disappeared. A child's awe as the chrysalis gradually blackened, became transparent like a stained glass window, and the new form was heralded as orange and black stripes became visible. Amazement as I watched the crumpled newness emerge, and gradually the wing veins pump to a stiffness like the putting up of an umbrella until they were ready for flight! I wondered about the experience of that tiny creature as its dissolution took place. How different from dying is the loss of every known thing? Some spark of life remained in the essence, I concluded, as skin and shape were shed and re-formed.

In the bush I fell in love with the tight-coiled bristly koru, and the way, as it released its brown tension, little green tendril fingers opened and hung vulnerably from the tentative growing. Then the bold, strong push to full fern-hood, the provision of shade, the base for the next generation of growth.

These days I am in awe at the transformation of my three grand-daughters aged two and three. From being adorable new babies they are now, in an astonishingly short time, small fully-functioning children, with distinct personalities, developing social and motor skills, a use of the English language which is astounding, the ability to make connections, recognition of the members of their large extended family, delicious senses of humour, and the capacity for consciously giving and receiving love. This has taken place without the degree of dissolution and the chaos in their lives that befalls a caterpillar. The chaos of birth is a major transforming event for the mother, and the baby's environment is changed, but for the baby there is still a continuity. After birth they are the same person with the same form as before.

Then there are the internal and external transformations in and around our own lives, that we cooperate with, or produce, or are a part of. Everyone has their own story to tell. We are not all Kate Shephards or Paulo Freires, having a major transforming influence for good on society, but as St Paul says: 'the life and death of each of us has its effect on others.'

My transformation project of the moment is the just-completed re-decoration of the house I moved into 12 months ago. It was so dark and dingy, even with its multiplicity of windows – brown everywhere, walls, floors, woodwork, tiles, stove; silver paper with a lime-green pattern on the chapel ceiling in the bathroom, with bath and basin of another green; the statutory orange kitchen sink-bench, all high fashion in the 1970s, but not my colours, even then. Persistence and diversions have both been as necessary as the paint-brushes, litres of white paint, and time spent finding colours that would sing to me. This physical change and lightening up has been an ongoing metaphor for the inner transformation experienced as I approach the end of several years of psychotherapy.

All the other sorts of transformations have been part of these journeys as both my inner and outer houses are being readied simply for living in and being enjoyed. I have been koru, caterpillar, chrysalis and tadpole, rain on the road, on the window, and sun-shaped in the sky. I have again been two, three and four years old – 'unless you become as a little child, you shall not enter ….' Each room of my 'real' house has had its parallels to parts of my inner journey. Some rooms have needed many re-visits as new materials came to hand or an extra coat of paint proved necessary. Sometimes it has been the slow, patient chipping-off of old tiles or tiny pieces of ugly wall-paper, the descent into often painful chaos on the way to a new place. It can be disorienting waking in a bedroom with a ladder up to its four-metre apex, furniture all pushed to one side, curtains replaced by a paint-splattered duvet cover, tools and paint pots stacked at the foot of the bed, the usual patterns of living disrupted or inaccessible. Sometimes what has felt daunting has gone surprisingly smoothly. Professional help has been necessary for what I could not do alone. The support of friends has been vital too. Both inner and outer transformations have been interwoven with the ordinary encounters and doings of daily life. Now the house is light, bright and lovely, some rooms restful, others with a touch of drama. And all mine!

These days new energy, and an appreciation of all that is, are flowing from the delight in how life is becoming, both its inner and outer aspects. Old patterns learned in a lifetime of excessive stress are losing their usefulness. I watch with joy as clouds diminish, rainbows appear more often and stay longer, a girl-child heals and matures, a tiny frog leaps back into its native water and discovers a new way to swim, koru unfurls in the sun, and multi-coloured wings strengthen for flight.

Community Care
– the Good News

We know it happens: the bad news makes the headlines and the good so often goes un-remarked upon. This seems to be particularly so in the area of mental health. The word 'Raurimu' sends shudders up spines as an example of community care gone wrong. There have been so many tragedies – but they are not the whole story. All is not well in that sector, and recent increases in funding may only help the overall picture in a small way. But the fact remains that a great deal of fine and successful work is being done in this area, and many people with long-term mental illness are leading lives that ten years ago they could scarcely have imagined. Two places where people's healing is furthered are Mana Community Enterprises (MCE) and Porch, both situated in Porirua City.

I have been chaplain at Mana Community Enterprises (Porirua) since 1999, and have been saddened at the negative media portrayals of mental health scenarios, which increase prejudice against those who have illnesses. This article was an attempt to redress the balance by highlighting the sound rehabilitation work being done by many dedicated professionals.

Liz is in a special position to understand the benefits of coming to the MCE workshop as part of rehabilitation from illness. She first came as a client in 1997 after a lifetime of trauma and abuse had led to a mental break-down. 'I thought I'd not be employed any more because of not being well, so I came to be a client at Mana hoping it would be a stepping-stone towards getting a job. After a while they saw my potential and I was encouraged to take a part-time position on the staff, then to study for my NZQA Certificate in Mental Health Care. I am now a qualified kai whakaruruhau (Māori counsellor). The professionalism I have learned has helped me be stronger and know my own mana, and help others know their mana too. So I'm an encouragement to others, particularly for my people who have been through so much. I tell them "if I can do it, so can you." Here they learn values and find out who they can trust. It's like a whānau. They know they are in a safe environment, and safety has been a rare commodity especially after the trauma of years in hospital. The aroha here is so important – it is a necessary part of their recovery. So for me MCE has been the biggest stepping-stone of all!'

MCE has two types of operation. One is a workshop in a warehouse where about thirty-five people with mental illnesses come to work. They are carefully assessed for their cognitive and physical capabilities and guided into tasks and projects that are appropriate to their skill and concentration levels. Some work is light assembly, for example, tea-light and birthday candle packaging, and cutting wall-paper samples. A recent big contract is sorting re-cycling materials for Porirua City Council and The Warehouse. Vailima, the outdoor section of MCE, has another thirty-five people involved in landscaping, lawns and nursery work. The work done is of high quality and any new work contracts are always welcome. The workers receive a token remuneration.

Over its 12-year existence, MCE management and staff have established an atmosphere and culture where everyone is respected, and social skills are instilled and insisted upon. In the corporate world 'a job' has many functions for employees: a structure for the day – a reason to get out of bed in the morning, a place where one's skills are valued, a locus for contributing to one's community, for social interaction and support, for learning new skills, and gaining some spending power. The same applies at MCE for these men and women, some of whom spent up to 40 years as patients in hospital. For some of the younger ones there is another factor – perhaps for the first time in their lives they are being consistently valued as human beings and treated with respect. Stories of horrific childhood abuse abound. Sometimes they saw illness-inducing drug-use as the only way available to survive.

By most 'ordinary' standards the lives of many of the workers are extraordinarily difficult: living with a life-pervading illness like depression or schizophrenia is hard enough, but there is also financial poverty, social marginalisation by the wider community, living under the scrutiny, and to some extent the control, of an assortment of medical practitioners and carers within the mental health system, and unpleasant side-effects of medications that make the illnesses more or less manageable. But coming to work is a powerfully therapeutic experience, where the prevailing atmosphere is cheerful and calm, there is a purpose in the activity, and people smile and are kind to each other.

Several of the workers from MCE and Vailima live at Porch. Russell and Tricia Fitzgerald established this residential care facility in the early 1990s when it became obvious that de-institutionalising of patients from Porirua Hospital was imminent. With their years of psychiatric nursing experience they were concerned for the future of patients they knew, some of whom had spent up to 50 years in hospital. Porch now boasts a new purpose-built complex which houses 20 long-term clients in motel-style units around a delightful courtyard. They and their staff provide 24-hour nursing care, monitor medication, and supervise and coach residents in self-care, social skills and budgeting. 'After so long in hospital, it can take years to learn the smallest things' said Tricia. 'We see a lot more self-respect now, a sense of belonging, and allowing themselves to trust.'

Another result of the move into the community, which excites Russell, is that some families have felt able to come back into clients' lives. 'They found going up that hospital driveway to visit too hard, but now they can visit family members here in just an ordinary way as equals.' He also credits improved medications with contributing to a quality of life some clients had not had for years.

Grant and Barbara, the client representatives at Porch, were unanimous in their enjoyment of their life there. Grant said, 'This is like a lovely castle – we're very lucky.' And from Barbara: 'They love me here – that's the main thing.' They were both involved in meetings with the local community in an effort to allay the fears of neighbours when Porch was being built. 'That was sad,' said Grant. 'We wouldn't hurt anyone.'

Part of the family atmosphere at Porch is doing what other families do – going for holidays. Recent expeditions have been to Queenstown and Bay of Islands. 'A huge exercise getting it all organised,' admits Russell, 'but so worthwhile seeing them enjoy all these new experiences.' A regular visitor to Porch is 'Pop,' Russell's father, Francis, who is appreciated like a grandad. He is a retired ambulance officer and has also known some of the clients for many years.

Healing (or in official terms, rehabilitation) does take place – usually by the millimetre. Many clients of both MCE and Porch have made visible progress over the last few years – in self-esteem, in connecting with others, and gaining skills that others take for granted. A few have moved on to more formal employment or into independent accommodation.

These two organisations provide valuable links in the mental health service and are truly places of Good News, though most who work there would not describe it in those terms. The clients are frequently awesome in their courage and cheerfulness and hopes for a better future, and the staff in their patience, good-humour, persistence, professional skills and clarity. There are two ways they all need the support of the wider community in order to maximise their work. Firstly, by an increase in society's acceptance of and respect for those who have a mental illness, so that 'out there' rehabilitation is enhanced not hampered. And secondly, MCE needs contracts for either intermittent or continuing work. Businesses who offer these not only make a contribution to the lives of some of God's anawim, they get a good job well done!

Ministering to Church Leavers 2002

There is a common perception among members of Christian churches that individuals who leave their church are doing so because they have 'lost their faith' and 'turned their backs' on both God and their community. In Catholic terms they have 'lapsed,' an exact equivalent of the evangelical term 'back-slidden.' Not necessarily so, says Dr Alan Jamieson, pastor at Wellington's Central Baptist Church.

> After my own painful experience as a 'church leaver,' I was moved by the work being done at Central Baptist Church, Wellington, and its origin in Dr Alan Jamieson's research.

His interest was sparked in the early nineties by observing that many people, whose integrity and commitment he respected, were leaving churches to which they had been deeply committed for a significant number of years. This led to his doctoral thesis and subsequent expansion of his findings into his book, *A Churchless Faith*[22] It also led to the establishment of a unique ministry to church leavers operated by Central Baptist. Known as Spirited Exchanges, this support group meets twice a month, and is facilitated by Jenny McIntosh, who leads this part-time paid ministry.

Alan's research findings were that most people who leave churches after intense commitment in fact continue to have a vibrant faith in God and Jesus. They simply cannot continue with integrity to express it in the setting/language/theological understanding/community in which they have hitherto done so. Spirited Exchanges gives such people a spiritual way-station with companionship and support from people who understand the pain of making such a move. There is space to reflect, voice doubts and fears, to be angry, to grieve for lost certainties.

Attendance at the group can be a dozen or more, said Jenny. The format is generally a discussion on an advertised topic, with sharing of personal journeys in smaller groups. Topics over the last year have included: Who is God? What is Prayer? Spiritual Abuse, Why I Left the Church, and Easter and the Absence of God. Other topics will be generated by the group.

Brenda, who has been with group for two years, said: 'When you leave the church you get really lonely, you miss the community. Here, there is acceptance with no agenda for you – no fear and no control. That feels amazing!' Another participant said, 'I don't have to watch my words here, and I'm only responsible for myself.'

For many, leaving their church can be a major life experience equating to divorce or bereavement. It throws up conflicts for the onlookers, too. Those who remain within the institution can feel threatened and rejected, and frequently find maintaining a relationship with the leaver in the too-hard basket, much as friends do after a divorce, despite the best intentions to remain in touch with both parties.

When Alan and Jenny addressed the national training event of the Association of Christian Spiritual Directors last year, they were asked whether they have an agenda for the people who come to the group. Did they see it as a way to gather up the lost sheep and return them to the fold? Their reply was engagingly honest: 'We used to see it like that, but now we don't. Now we understand that leaving a (or the) church is a valid and necessary part of some people's spiritual journeys. They may or may not join another denomination, but the God-journey is going to continue.'

Alan makes a strong correlation of his findings with Fowler's stages of faith, and concludes that most Evangelical, Pentecostal, Charismatic (EPC) churches on which his research focussed are geared to people with up to stage 3 faith. Stage 3 is characterised by Fowler as needing external authority/a parental figure, with followers grouped around a leader. In contrast, Alan assesses the general level of New Zealand secular society to be at stage 4 level, where self-responsibility, plurality and listening to all the voices are becoming the norm. Question: does the Catholic umbrella offer room for the development of more stages of faith than EPC churches? Catholics are far less homogeneous in theology than, say, Assemblies of God members.

So is it worth taking, this huge step of faith in one's faith journey, leaving the familiar church? Can God really be 'in the other place'? Does God roam free of the boundaries of denomination and institutional religion? Is there really 'nowhere else to go'? Spirited Exchanges provides food and shelter for the early part of the journey out into the desert away from the companionship of those with whom the travellers have pitched their tents for a long time. Some join another denomination. Many find their way later to a group of people whose journey has taken them down a similar track. These post-church faith groups are the topic of Alan's latest research.

A recent analysis by US Catholic sister, Sandra Schneiders, has it that by abandoning their religious institution, individuals lose the influence that would enable them to bring about change in either church or society, have no access to the shared practice of a time-tested tradition, no longer enjoy the wisdom of the great figures of the tradition or a coherent theology, no longer experience the nourishment of a canonical sacred literature, and have no access to the tested traditions of moral ideals and restraints. Again, not so, say Alan and Jenny – church leavers can take with them the best of their learnings, including moral ideals, and continue to make a contribution to bettering the society in which they live.

While the compassionate work that is being done by Central Baptist is focussed mainly on people leaving EPC churches, this ministry raises questions for Catholic parishes. What happens to priests and other parishioners when someone indicates being unsettled or starts talking about leaving? Is there a willingness to try to understand, to continue in ministry to that person, to wish them well, to have confidence that God is with them and still guiding their way? Could there be a farewell ritual, even a viaticum – food for the journey? If corporate bodies conduct exit interviews in an attempt to refine their business practice, what useful information could the church learn from those who are departing? Is there an emphasis, shared with EPC churches, on bringing people in the front door (for example, through the Right of Christian Initiation of Adults (RCIA) programme) while resolutely ignoring those leaving by the back door? Thirty years ago there was a sense that God never led people out of the Catholic Church. Has this changed?

As Alan writes in *A Churchless Faith*, in a plea for leaver-sensitive churches: 'Church leavers tell their horror stories … surely this cannot be a good advertisement for the Christian faith. Putting time and effort into leavers may not lead them to come back, but it can significantly reduce the negativity of their experience and their stories.'

And if God is truly known as having a special care for the marginalised, how might the Catholic Church en-flesh this care for those whose journey leads them to its margins and beyond?

Celebrating Susanna

'There's a ravening tiger inside me and it's eating me up.' The woman had just disclosed to a counsellor for the first time that she had been sexually abused by a clergyman. She was startled by the counsellor's next question: 'Can you find a name for the tiger?' A deep, puzzled silence, then she 'knew' the tiger's name was Susanna. A very odd name for a tiger, especially as she knew no-one with that name! Where had it come from? Perhaps it was a biblical name…

A reprise of the Susanna story, which had been such an important resource for me and other women. Time to record interventions and achievements.

Back home she checked the biographical list in the back of the family Bible and was stunned to discover the story of Susanna in the book of Daniel. A story that had many parallels to her own. The story of a woman condemned because of the honourable reputations of her would-be seducers. In the shock of recognition she knew too that this was a God-moment. Her God had drawn her attention to this story, and was, she sensed, as firmly on her side as on Susanna's all those millennia ago!

She told this story the following year when she'd become part of a group of women survivors of sexual abuse by clergy who had begun meeting for mutual support. The catalyst for the group had been a conference addressing the topic in Palmerston North in October 1992. On hearing her story they immediately decided that their group should bear Susanna's name. The women were from a variety of denominations, and had not always been abused within their own. The ages at which they had been abused also varied. The common ground was the pain – deep, long-lasting, and damage – emotional, psychological, physical, financial and, not least, spiritual.

In the ten years since that Palmerston North gathering, when the unspeakable was spoken, there has been some progress in the churches in dealing with sexual abuse by their ministers. It is by no means a new problem: a decree was passed by the Roman emperor about 370 AD forbidding clergy to visit the homes of widows and virgins!

And Susanna Group has contributed to that recent progress in all sorts of ways. Members have attended international conferences on sexual abuse by clergy and health professionals in Australia in 1996 and 1998, and brought back for interested parties the latest information from specialist professionals on dealing with victims/survivors, perpetrators and affected parishes. As a group they have critiqued the draft protocols or procedures that various churches began producing, and have served on complaints committees of two denominations.

A major feature on sexual abuse by clergy in the June 1997 *Crosslink*, the former Presbyterian/Methodist paper, was based on Susanna Group contributions. This particular issue won international acclaim.

Susanna Group has issued various press releases since 1994, calling among other things for naming of offenders, the compilation by the Catholic Church of full statistics of offending clergy and religious, and the appointment of an ombudsman for church affairs. At last it seems that progress is being made in some of these areas, in the Catholic context at least.

They have 'spoken the truth to power' and it has, with a few exceptions, not been welcomed at the time. But ultimately, now that the courageous men who have also been abused by clergy and religious have spoken out, the tide seems to have turned. In itself that is a point to ponder! Susanna Group is grateful to those few clergy and lay people who have educated themselves effectively on the issues involved, and have become part of this most difficult ministry: hearing of complaints, dealing with perpetrators, with distraught and conflicted parishes, and with the media.

But the heart of the Susanna Group has been the healing companionship the women have offered each other and others who have made contact over the years. They have not needed the overseas research which demonstrates that contact with others who have had this same experience is beneficial. There really is nothing like the understanding offered by someone who has 'been there'!

The women have also supported each other in many ways through their individual complaint processes. These have by and large been frustrating, and not infrequently traumatic to the point of re-abuse. If your main reason for exposing your pain to the authorities is to prevent the same thing happening to anyone else, then they prove obtuse, toothless or both, it can be very soul-destroying! And another service was to the brave wife of an abusing clergyman, helping to get her story into the public eye in *Crosslink,* June 1999.

Women have stayed in touch with the group for varying lengths of time according to their need. One member says: 'When I talk with other Susanna members, I know I am heard. I don't have to explain the context, give detailed analyses, or "educate", as I do with friends, however well-meaning, who don't share the same pain. It is also special to share our joys, our progress, our victories – and to delight in the good we find in each other and in our world.'

For most, the present prospect of a safer church comes too late: they have found it impossible to do the necessary healing within an institution where those who abused them remained in ministry, and understanding of their predicament among other members of the parish community is minimal. They have gone out into the desert where many discover in their various ways that truly 'God is in the other place.'

But at least now they have some sense that they are being vindicated, just as the biblical Susanna was when her community eventually realised the full truth of what had been happening.

Another Response to Jacquie's Daughter, Maybe for When She's a Little Older

2003

A Catholic mother wrote an article for *Tui Motu InterIslands*, grieving that she'd had to explain to her 10-year old daughter why she could not be a priest. This was my heart-felt response. It found a home in *Vashti's Voices*.

I wonder what you think being a priest is all about. One way to describe it is that it is about tending people with the love and respect of Jesus for their uniqueness, and putting them in touch with God, especially at important moments in their lives, like births and deaths and marriages. And in a special way being authorised to offer Jesus to the community and to God through the Eucharist.

Guess what, sweet-heart – you may never be ordained by the church to say mass, but you are already a priest. You really truly are! St Peter, writing to some of the early Christian communities – not just to its leaders – said: 'You are a chosen race, a royal priesthood, a people set apart.' By your baptism you belong to the 'priesthood of all believers,' though we haven't heard that phrase often in recent years. Our Anglican friends have a version of it which excited me when I first heard it: 'the ordination of baptism.' Our baptism authorises us all – women and men – to minister in the name of Jesus.

When I was pondering the role of the ordained priesthood a long time ago, it occurred to me that Mary, Jesus' mother, was the first real priest of the Christian tradition. She received Jesus as a gift from God, made him available to the community of the world, and ultimately on Calvary (as I understood it then) offered him back to his Father. Surely that made her a priest! I then discovered that Mechthild of Magdeburg had had a vision of Mary in priestly vestments back in the 13th century. Women have been thinking about these things for a long time!

Another, whose reflections have taken her down this track, is Frances Croake Frank (quoted in *Vashti's Voices*, Autumn 2003).

> Did the woman say,
> When she held him for the first time in the dark of a stable,
> After the pain and the bleeding and the crying
> 'This is my body, this is my blood'?

> Did the woman say,
> When she held him for the last time in the dark rain on a hilltop,
> After the pain and the bleeding and the dying,
> 'This is my body, this is my blood'?

Well that she said it to him then,
For dry old men,
Brocaded robes belying barrenness,
Ordain that she not say it for him now.

While we are touching on sacraments,[23] even the current laws of the church leave a door open for your priesthood. Baptism can in an emergency be administered by anyone; as a woman you may distribute the Eucharist; when you marry your loved one, you will each administer the sacrament of matrimony to each other – the ordained priest is a witness; God responds to the ministry of lay people when they pray for the release of the power of the Holy Spirit in people's lives, and pray with and anoint the sick, as is done with confirmation and sacrament of the sick. And reconciliation is the formal pronouncement that God has already forgiven us. So that only leaves ordination, which absolutely needs an ordained priest/bishop to administer it.

Another way that ordination is understood by some women, and some men too, is that it is intended to confer on men the sensitivity and gifts for giving appropriate (that is, truly helpful and healing) spiritual and emotional care at major life moments; in a way, to catch them up with what women can already do. Maybe this is one reason why many gay men are ordained and make good priests. They often seem to have an innate sensitivity beyond that of their heterosexual peers. And those of the latter who are honourable priests have my deep respect.

It is a mystery where the men 'in charge' believe their authority 'to allow' or 'not allow' women's ministry comes from in the first place (that is, historically). The Jesus of the gospels not only allowed women to minister, he allowed them to minister to him personally. If, as was believed for centuries, sin entered the world through women, and they really are 'temples built over sewers' (Tertullian and others), that could perhaps justify banning them from ordination. Jesus apparently did not share this opinion! And times have moved on. Such condemnations are no longer heard, but the consequent exclusion is ferociously retained!

What about the old story that women cannot be ordained because only men were present at the Last Supper, as per Leonardo de Vinci's painting, where the sacrament of ordination was instituted? Wrong again! This was a Passover meal that they sat down to that evening, a Seder in the Jewish tradition, where women and children are an integral part of the ritual.

So there you are: most of what priesthood is about is already available to you. Claim it! Do not leave it to men 'to allow' or 'disallow' your ministry. Develop your prayer-life. Do whatever theological and pastoral care training seems right. Exercise your priesthood as and where your God calls you. It will very likely be outside the institutional church, unless you are very good at keeping rules, and don't mind 'passing it over to Father' at a crucial moment when you have done the spadework of relationship-building.

And remember the Eucharist 'happens' in other contexts: as you share a meal with friends and you are aware of the love among you; as someone shares the story of a life broken open and you bear witness to it; when as maybe a marriage or funeral celebrant you touch into sacred moments with people who do not want the institution and its requirements for themselves on these occasions. The formal sacraments are meant to point us towards the sacred in everyday life. And so they do – but it is possible to 'go direct'!

Every person you will ever encounter has a spirituality. They may not call it that, but God is an experienced under-cover agent. When people speak of 'Nature' or 'the Universe' or 'the Divine,' the God you worship at mass is alive and well in their lives. You may well be the one, the priest, who ministers the love and respect of Jesus to them at their crucial ('cross'/'transition') moments.

There are many Catholic and formerly-Catholic women who would have jumped at priestly ordination if it had been offered them ten years ago. And they were ready, sufficiently theologically and pastorally educated to do so. Most of these, having watched the straws in the wind, and having seen the struggles of ordained women in other denominations, would now if offered ordination say 'no thank-you,' and continue exercising their priesthood as they understand it, wherever their God-journey takes them.

Dancing with Gratitude 2004

When one lives inside a culture it is often impossible to tell that one is doing so! Life simply has norms and givens that are shared with those around, taken for granted, and believed to be 'normal.' To have lived as Catholic Christian is to have been part of a culture, and I have been realising recently how an almost lifetime in this culture has made distinctive contributions to my life.

Recognising the richly formative influences of having been a Catholic...

I'm not talking about the conscious 'God-seeking' that is obviously the prime purpose of the whole exercise. Anyway, there are so many ways of doing this as a Christian and Catholic, that those with whom my journey has significant common ground may not be a large proportion of the whole. But there are three significant 'subliminal' areas of which I have recently become very aware that are universally shared: community, the liturgical cycle, and the use of symbolism and metaphor. I recognise God-at-work in our lives through these experiences as well. And I'm more deeply aware now of the good things that have come my way.

There's the basic parish community ethos: if there's a birth, go; if there's an illness, go; if there's been a death, go; if there's a celebration, go! There was the parish roster to take me to hospital daily to visit my premature baby when we had no car. When my husband died suddenly, people came, came in staggering numbers. I didn't know we knew so many! They came with gifts of food and tactfully-offered money. The parish women took over the afternoon tea at my home after the funeral – the parish urn and crockery and more mountains of food appeared. I didn't have to do a thing – it was all quietly and compassionately 'seen to.' The next week a friend sent her husband up with their motor-mower to do the by-then shaggy lawns.

And some sense of entitlement to ask for help: I'll always bless the parish friend who came in response to my frantic phone call at 11.30 pm on Christmas Eve, the first after my husband had died. I'd bought the six year-old a second-hand bike which was in great condition, but when it was brought out from its hiding place under the house one tyre was flat! It wouldn't have been a happy way to get it, even with tales of puncture by reindeer-antlers! It was duly mended, received with Christmas morning excitement, and subsequently maintained for a few years by the same man. All this kindness, amazing at the time, and still a huge memory! I learned that it can often be more blessed to receive than to give; and that it is rarely possible to repay kindness, but it is possible to 'pass it on.' And, yes, I have at times been involved with others in their times of need. The ties from those years are still strong.

Then there is the annual liturgical cycle – Advent, Christmas, Lent, Easter, Pentecost, Ordinary time, and then Advent again. I hadn't realised how deeply this had become part of my psyche until I worshipped in a setting where this Holy Spiral is not observed. And in the background beyond formal liturgy is its connection to the earth's cycle. It is much easier to connect with the original meanings in the Northern hemisphere, as Christmas was the Light coming into the darkest time, and Easter truly coincides with the new life of Spring. In Aotearoa New Zealand we have to use our imaginations and adapt: our Christmas is a celebration of the presence of warmth and the Son/Sun. Our Easter is a time of planting and promise of new life sprouting in the tomb-darkness of the approaching winter. And Pentecost is our fire festival of new hope and courage in the darkness of the year. And so we participate in rituals, in some respects not so very different from those of the countless generations who celebrated their wonder and hope in the millennia before the Christian era.

And among that cycle we remember the anniversaries of deaths and births and weddings: and feast-days celebrate year by year those whose memories are cherished in the universal community, and in more local areas. None of this is news – but, perhaps along with many, I had taken it all for granted. Now I see it as a precious gift which has year by year harmonised my being with the earth and the community, as well as with the cycle of the Christ-story.

Recently I recognised another jewel of a gift from this Catholic Christian culture when someone commented on my facility with symbol and metaphor. Surprised, I wondered where this could have come from. It didn't take long to realise that this, too, comes from the same source: the community of faith has metaphor and symbol as a primary tool of communication. These are simply the shared language in which we express beliefs and truths and understandings.
We speak of the journey of faith, of deserts, of exodus, of crucifixions and resurrections. The gospels, no less than the Hebrew Scriptures, are a veritable compendium of metaphors – Jesus is Living Bread, Living Water, Living Word, the Way, the Truth, the Life. So many words bring their stories with them: we all know the significance of rainbows, of guiding stars, of Job's comforters, and the images of the 23rd Psalm.

How enriched our language, our common understandings, our lives are with all these images! Being taught to think and pray and describe life in these ways has been a fabulous gift which I am just beginning to really appreciate. It had not occurred to me that not everyone has access to all this treasure! Yet with Aquinas we eventually recognise that *all* God-language is metaphor – no words can contain the Mystery! In St Paul's famous metaphor for human understanding, 'we see through a glass darkly.' With this recognition comes a new freedom in the naming of the Divine, and the ultimate need for simple silence.

So I am dancing with gratitude that these three wonderful strands of life have been woven into the fabric of my being. I can't imagine who or how I would be without them! To my Catholic ancestors, to the parish of Northland/Wilton, Wellington, which was my home, my community and language-nest for 30 years, to teachers, retreat facilitators and spiritual directors, to my companions-in-faith – for these three precious gifts, thank you and thank you and thank you!

The Table Ministry of Jesus 2005

It happened again! At a requiem mass for the second time in a month in two different dioceses I again did some dying myself. Priest number one said: 'Communion is for Catholics who receive the Eucharist regularly. Others please generously remain in your seats and pray for our friend.' Priest number two, at the relevant point in an otherwise deeply moving liturgy, said: 'Catholics may receive Communion, and people of other faiths are welcome to come forward for a blessing.'

> The Eucharist has always been vitally important to me, and its deep meaning, the uniting and the including.

It is many years since I first heard the term 'the Table Ministry of Jesus.' Initially it didn't mean a lot. In fact it sounded to my Catholic ears a rather Protestant term! However, as I listened further to an inspired set of video lectures on Christology by Dr Anthony Moore from Georgetown University, it started to become clear. And not just clear, but recognisably the crucial centre-piece of what Jesus came to tell us.

The Table Ministry is about those with whom Jesus chose to eat, namely the prostitutes, tax-collectors and other outcasts from his community. He opted to share his life and meals with the team at the bottom of the league. And warned those who thought they had it together, the scribes and Pharisees, that they actually were missing the point, and would themselves be found at the bottom of the league when it came to admission to everlasting life.

It wasn't just that Jesus came as a respectable Jew to eat with the anawim, the lowly ones: as his ministry unfolded he actually became one of their number in reality. He became an outcast himself. The establishment could not handle his calls for truth and justice. People turned against him. He was condemned as a criminal. He spent his dying hours hung naked from a cross, sharing the fate of other common criminals. He lived to the fullest and deepest the Beatitudes, those nonsensical reversals of all the values that 'normal' people hold dear. From that basis he gained his street credibility. He knows what it is like at the bottom of the heap.

How often I have heard Sunday sermons extolling the God of the marginalised: 'If you want to meet God, go to the marginalised people.' When it comes to the Eucharistic table, what would Jesus do? He would invite, include. What does the organisational church do? It discriminates, excludes. The church by this and various other rule-makings actively marginalises people.

Does it listen to its own teaching about where God is to be found? Does it go to the anawim it has created and say, 'Show us your God'?

The Eucharist is at the very heart of what Jesus gave and gives. If the way in which this is shared, or not, is out of line with the core of his teaching, how can the rest hold together? There are some courageous priests who say on such occasions: 'All are welcome to receive communion.' There are more circumspect ones who say nothing and leave the decision to the faith and conscience of the individuals. But sadly there are many who take on the role of active excluder.

A woman who was at one of these funerals, an ordained person in her own Christian denomination, said she would have valued receiving communion in remembrance of her friend. When she heard 'those of other faiths' could receive a blessing, she wondered whether there were Buddhists present. Then the penny dropped, 'He meant me!' She did not go forward. There were others hurt by the exclusion, too, all the more poignantly as this funeral celebrated the life of someone who had worked ecumenically over a long period.

One of my most precious Eucharistic experiences was with a Protestant minister and a man who had AIDS. As we shared bread and cup I knew the intense reality of the presence of Jesus with us. Sacramental Eucharist points us to the moments of sharing and communion in our ordinary lives. How will we recognise these if we are comfortable eating the Christ-meal in front of others who have been told they may not eat? On more than one such occasion I have remained in my seat in solidarity with the pain of the excluded ones. And I have wondered, too, whether there is a gender difference in perception of these exclusions. Women, as the traditional preparers and servers of meals, know in their bones that to prepare and serve a meal, then announce who may and may not eat is just plain wrong.

Eucharist is a sign that we are each sufficiently poor and marginalised to be among Jesus' preferred table companions ('breakers of bread together'). How then can others be excluded as being less worthy than ourselves? If God entrusted Jesus to the human race and was prepared to redeem the consequences, how is it that the sacramental Presence has to be guarded so vehemently to prevent any risk of its Reality being misunderstood? Is this out-Godding God?

Imagine: there is a special mass being said with many present from other denominations and other faiths. The priest makes one of the excluding statements, which boils down to 'only Catholics qualify to receive communion.' While the Catholics queue in the aisles to receive the sacramental Jesus from the priest, those left in the pews are suddenly aware of the presence of the living human Jesus at the back of the church. He moves among these marginalised ones, sharing and healing their hurt, giving them Holy Food and talking personally with each one. Those of all beliefs and none respond to his loving concern for them. The Catholics return to their seats and suddenly realise they have been missing something. When after few moments an appalled new awareness dawns, Jesus the Includer touches each of them as well. And then he moves to the front – and embraces the priest…

Psychotherapy as Sacrament

I little knew when I was drawn to the caving journey in 1992 ('In Deep') what a powerful metaphor it would become for the psychotherapy journey I embarked on in 1996. I was still then suffering from post-traumatic stress disorder from the clergy abuse and abusive complaint processes, and wanted to get it out of my system once and for all.

This is the first of only two pieces written specifically for this book as a necessary back-drop to the journey so far. It is about some very important stitchings-together of recent years.

L. had been my supervisor as I did my counselling training in 1994-95, and I had related deeply to her style of working with me. I wanted to avail myself of her skills for my own benefit. And so a long journey began. A few of the poems of this journey have appeared earlier in the book ('Seeing,' 'Starting,' 'Therapy'). As with the Lost World caving expedition, both terrors and miracles have abounded, and at times on this journey, too, especially near its end, when I've needed the support of other friends as well as my guide.

I'd been horrified to hear at the Sydney Conference in 1996 that some women needed up to ten years of therapy to recover from the experience of sexual abuse by clergy. If I'd known at the outset that mine would be a nine-year venture I would never have started! Long – yes, slow – yes, but at my own pace, and so respectful and so organic! No precipitating techniques, simply the therapist's confidence that nature would take its course, and that this model of therapy would give me a solid foundation for the rest of my life. And that work became tūrangawaewae, my place to stand, the place where I was 'heard into speech.'

There was so much healing to do through so many layers and decades of life. In a dream early on I descended again into the bowels of the earth as I'd done at Lost World, but the sides of this tomo (shaft) were all grey and solidly concreted over, desecrated! No sign of the beautiful mosses, ferns and creepers of the real-life expedition! And that was how my necessary defence mechanisms had affected my emotional life. Removing the concrete has been hard work; sometimes patiently, a fragment at a time, at other times great hunks coming away in explosions. In another dream I needed to dive to the bottom of a deep, deep pool to recover a small drowned child, then resuscitate her.

No-one had ever before worked at understanding me as consistently, deeply and compassionately. This dynamic, and being given week by week safe space in which to become and discover my Self, to feel old fears, and try new ways of relating was a powerfully healing experience. I drew artistically inexpert stick figure illustrations on my way through the years as an extra way to communicate my inner world. The early pictures abound with boxes with frightened eyes peering from beneath the lids, and later on, cliff edges. It was a significant moment when I drew a box big enough for two people: I was eventually convinced of L's willingness to know what my inner world was like, for as long as the healing would take.

A sacrament is, by the old catechism definition, 'an outward sign of inward grace,' and over time I recognised the deeply sacramental nature of this work. Throughout my life-journey God, Jesus and the Holy Spirit have been present, and at times have actively healed me in my spirit/psyche. There have been many occasions during the therapy where such a gift 'in the spirit' has been played out in the embodied human realm, by daylight, so to speak. These were the 'outward signs,' the earthing, the embodiment in the human realm, of 'inward graces,' of prayer insights and experiences, such as those described in the first part of 'About Loving' and 'Straightening.' The therapist has had the tenacious patience I attributed to Jesus, and took the stance of close listening he offered to the woman who was bent double when he knelt to hear her.

Much later I recognised the nature of the sacred commitment that the therapist silently makes to the client at the beginning of therapy. L. described herself as 'not a believer,' but one day as we talked of the nature of her role, she used the word 'agape' to describe her stance. And that is what I understand as simply Christ-love, even if it is not recognised or named as such.

I knew from the beginning that God wanted for me the healing I wanted for myself, and that to work for this with another human being, rather than solely in prayer, was the call, the struggle and the gift. Because this was two human beings working together, there have been mistakes and unintentional hurts. Working through these, redeeming them, has been fruitful.

Therapy has been my Way of the Cross repeated in so many variations, so often. So often the familiar sequence of Friday agonies, Saturday numbness and Sunday Resurrection joy has been the template that has kept me from despair, as yet another layer of pain and fear became evident. And the human embodied experience has borne out the Easter reality. After each crisis and its resolution has come the new energy, freedom and clarity that make it all worthwhile.

Another metaphor, which has had profound significance for me, has been that of labouring towards a new birth, with my God and the therapist as mid-wives. There has been an eventual re-birth of the whole and holy child who was displaced and misplaced in early childhood. The labour was long and intense, the human mid-wife skilled, experienced and totally present.

I wondered at intervals whether this journey was self-indulgent. I knew, and know still, that it was an enormous gift and privilege. There are plenty of others who could claim greater need than mine. But then the understanding prevailed that 'The glory of God is a human being fully alive' (Irenaeus). And that attending to myself and my inner ecology is a key (but not the only) part of my contribution to world peace. The inner healing removes blocks to effective living and loving.

And there was the retreat poster years ago: 'The longest journey is within.' I have made this pilgrimage! Where has God been along the way? She is the Ground of our Being – I have some understanding of that phrase now! She is where we go deep and do our emotional archaeology in order to straighten that which was crooked and make level the paths for our future energy and creativity. She is the Ground our roots penetrate for nourishment. She has held us both in Her hands, rejoicing at the progress, weeping over the terrors and pain. She has been the therapeutic relationship, the Verb, the essence of 'what happens between us.' She is there still, now that the active therapy relationship is ended. She has given and contained this extraordinary time of healing and the relationship that made it possible. Thanks be to Her!
And her, both!

And Now...

This particular patchwork is now backed, bound, quilted and ready for giving away. The longer story, though, is unfinished. With contentment and a sense of wholeness, this is a good place to pause. I look forward to discovering the future! What is contained in this book is not the entire story – many writings have not been included, many aspects of life have not been written about. As happens, not all available fabrics have been used in this project. They and the left-over fragments will be there for another time.

I treasure my friends. They are all amazing, gifted, sensitive people, and I am so blessed to have this chosen whānau around me. They have been with me in good times and bad. Without them I may not have survived. With one, last week, I had a celebratory latte marking fifty years of friendship; several others go back forty-five years. And the newer ones are precious too!

Externally, life has mostly been very ordinary. There have been the Playcentre, kindergarten, school and other committees, the night-classes, friendships, various part-time jobs, precious times spent with children and grandchildren, times back in Tauranga, my New Zealand home-town, two trips to Europe. There have been adventures with friends over the last few years: Milford Track, canoeing the Whanganui River, a hot-air balloon ride, Abel Tasman National Park, the Tongariro Crossing. And a year at art school in 2004. There will be more challenges!

I have heard a number of older women say 'your sixties are the best time of your life.' This may well be so! It is certainly an interesting vantage point from which to be able to look back two generations in one direction, then ahead to the next two. It is fascinating to see some of the family features and traits appearing in my wonderful grandchildren!

There have been many learnings. Here are some that are important now:

Life is like a smorgasbord – it is impossible to have/know/do it all. Choices have to be made.

There are at least as many people with a deep and healthy spirituality outside the formal church structures as there are within.

There is no such thing as objectivity. Quantum physics bears this out. It is a patriarchal fantasy!

Theological truths are always seen and applied through the lens of individual life stories.

Whatever we discover is for the benefit of the community, not just ourselves.

Pleasure has its special holiness.

Anger heals.

God is a Shape-Shifter who says 'Who, where, do you need me to be?'

Behind the linguistics, metaphors and contexts, all who worship the Good, all who look beyond themselves, are aligned to the same Reality.

The entirety of creation is permeated with this Presence. All is sacred.

When I gave up on atonement theology that was a huge relief! Yes, Jesus was crucified, that much is history. But I am no longer able to attribute that to a God who demanded a blood-sacrifice. My understanding now is that when someone stands up for Truth and Justice against the establishment, it is the establishment that does the crucifying. It happened to the prophets.
It happened to Jesus. It happens still. The Resurrection, as it reiterates the story of the seasonal cycle and the old myths, is the fundamental message of hope and regeneration to individuals and communities.

I have a sense that the religious metaphors and teachings that are dearest to us are those that best match our psychological state and the life-wounds we have incurred. They can heal and they can harm! Asking 'is this belief/ideal/story life-giving?' is a crucial check.

The One in whose womanly image I am made still plays the key role in my life, though yes, essentially the Divine is beyond gender. Jesus is there as Friend and Brother. Love, justice, truth-seeking, peace-making and care for the planet through simplicity of life-style, are my core values. There is still much learning and growing to do!

My feminism came primarily from my reading of the gospels and Jesus' respect for women, and in particular his promise to 'proclaim liberty to the captives ... and set the down-trodden free.' (Luke 4: 18). Only subsequently did the common ground become apparent with all who are passionate about the well-being of women. I can vouch for the truth that 'the personal becomes political,' and that 'the political' of necessity includes 'the personal'!

ExAlt, a women's spirituality group, has been my ongoing community for the last few years. It began in an Anglican church in 1993 to raise consciousness of violence against women in Christian contexts, though I did not participate for another couple of years. In 2000 we moved to a secular building, as we'd been deemed 'not Christian enough' to remain in that parish. The group is non-hierarchical, and any one or two of us work on a voluntary basis to shape the monthly gathering. These are variously known as celebrations, rituals or offerings. A topic is chosen and a framework set up so that each person who attends has a space for her own thoughts and feelings. Most of us have had deep involvement in our churches, and then needed to leave. Ministry continues there and elsewhere.

At seventeen, I hypothesised the unity of all truth – that whatever is true somehow fits with whatever else is true. I have been reminded of this recently as I have recognised a convergence in the various strands of women's spirituality. I hear church and ex-church women speaking of the Divine using precisely the same words as women who describe themselves as pagans or as process philosophers who relate to the Goddess. Where might this take us? How will this weave together?

My patchwork and collage are tangible ways of collecting fragments and fitting them together into a bigger design. This book too has been a patchwork exercise, each 'patch' with its own internal patch-working dynamics as experiences, theory, reflection and response all informed each other into some sort of coherence. Coherence – that is a deeply satisfying word for me! And when more information arrives, the current picture may have to be dismantled yet again, to a greater or lesser degree, to incorporate it!

A couple of weeks ago I walked round the area of our original home for the first time in years. It was a scintillating Wellington winter's day. The view is still amazing. Our front bank, laboriously cleared of gorse forty years ago, is now covered with regenerating bush. The trees on the path and roadsides are taller. The park where my children played is still there. The kingfishers still flash turquoise, tūīs with golden throats still celebrate the winter sun. It is forty-two years since I went there as a bride, thirty-one since we moved on to the bigger home. It has been an eventful and blessed time. Without all that has happened, I would not have got to here! God is faithful. God is good. God is love.

All shall be well, and all shall be well, and every manner of thing shall be well!

Julian of Norwich

Appendix 1 — Summary of J W Fowler's Stages of Faith[24]

Each stage has characteristic ways of engaging with seven modes: Form of Logic – Form of World Coherence – Role-Taking – Locus of Authority – Bounds of Social Awareness – Forms of Moral Judgement – Role of Symbols.

NB: No stage is any more 'meritorious' than any other.

Stage			Age (approx)
1	Intuitive-projective	Faith from parents (moods and actions)	0–6
2	Mythic-literal	Faith from parents/parent substitute ('stories')	7–12
3	Synthetic-conventional	Faith from environment (group)	13–?
4	Individuative-reflexive	Individuals begin to be responsible for their own faith (polarities arise)	?16–?
5	Conjunctive or Paradoxical-consolidative	Individuals absorb good from opposite polarities	?30–?
6	Universalising	Resolution/Superanimation of all polarities	?38–?

Appendix 2 — Power and Equality Wheels

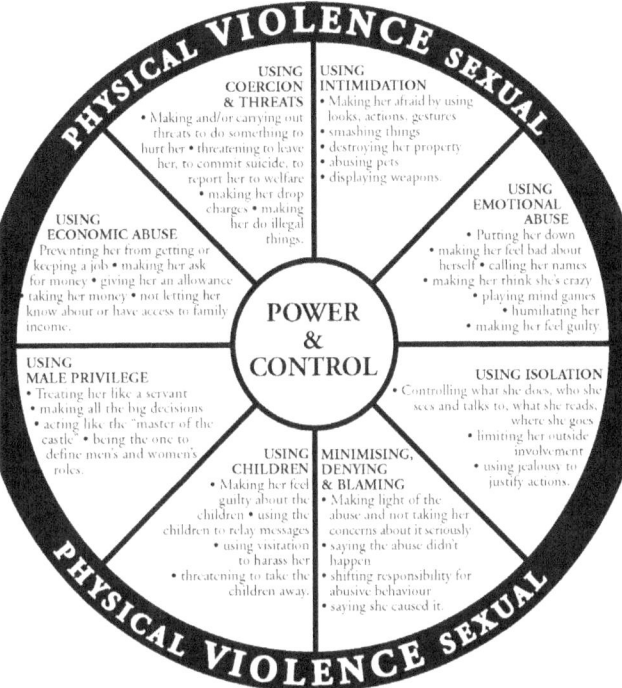

National Collective of Independent Women's Refuges Inc.

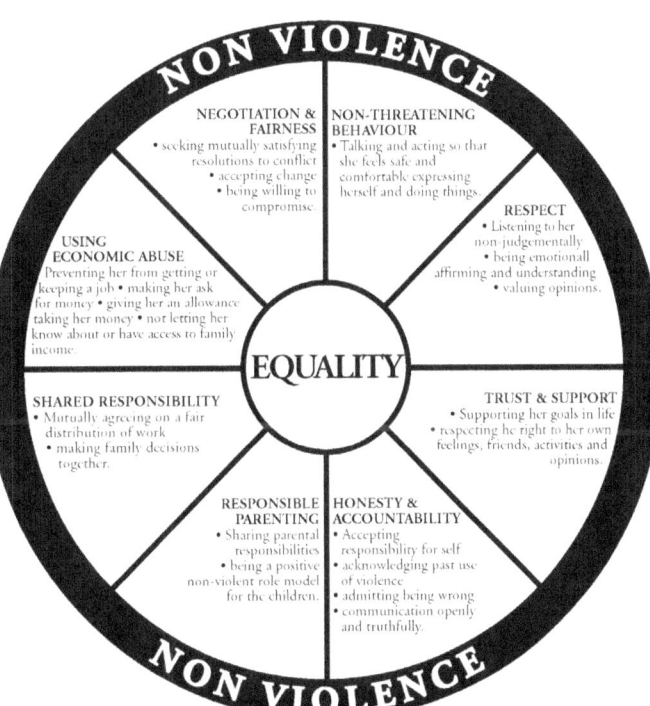

National Collective of Independent Women's Refuges Inc.

Selected Bibliography

Bass, Ellen, and Davis, Laura (1990) *The Courage to Heal*. Cedar, London

Batten, Juliet (1995) *Celebrating Southern Seasons, Rituals for Aotearoa*. Tandem Press, North Shore City

Bromell, David, Donnelly, Felix, Hein, Willem, Neave, Rosemary (1991) *Love Unbounded: on being Gay, or Lesbian and Christian*. Colcom Press, Hibiscus Coast, New Zealand

Christ, Carol P (1995) 3rd edition. *Diving Deep and Surfacing: Women Writers on Spiritual Quest*. Beacon Press, Boston, US

Christ, Carol P (2004) *She Who Changes – Re-imagining the Divine in the World*. Palgrave, Basingstoke

Cotter, Jim (1987) *Healing, More or Less*. Cairns Publications, Sheffield

Dale, Judith (1994) 'Christology.' In *Women and Church Shaping the Future*. 4th National Feminist Theology Conference, Women's Resource Centre, Auckland

Dominian, Jack (1981) *Marriage, Faith and Love*. Darton, Longman Todd, London

Douglas, Kay (1994) *Invisible Wounds – a self-help guide for New Zealand women in destructive relationships*. Penguin, Auckland

Estes, Clarissa Pinkola (1994) *Women Who Run With the Wolves*. Random House, Auckland

Fiorenza, Elisabeth Schuessler (1983) *In Memory of Her*. Crossroad, New York

Fortune, Marie (1989) *Is Nothing Sacred? When Sex Invades the Pastoral Relationship*. Harper and Row, San Francisco

Fowler, James W (1995) *Stages of Faith: the Psychology of Human Development and the Quest for Meaning*. Harper. San Francisco

Fox, Matthew (1983a) *Original Blessing*. Bear and Co, Santa Fe, US

Fox, Matthew (1983b) *Meditations with Meister Eckhardt*. Bear and Co, Santa Fe, US

Frankl, Viktor E (1959) *Man's Search for Meaning*. Simon and Schuster, New York

Freire, Paulo (1972) *The Pedagogy of the Oppressed*. Penguin (NZ), Auckland

Kelsey, Morton (1972) *Encounter with God – A Theology of Christian Experience*. Bethany House, Bloomington, US

Gage, Matilda Joslyn (1980) Reprint of 1893 original. *Women, Church and State, the Original Expose of Male Collaboration Against the Female Sex*. Persephone Press, Massachusetts

Gateley, Edwina (1990) *I Hear a Seed Growing*. Source Books, Trabuco Canyon, US, and Anthony Clarke Books, Wheathampstead, UK

Grace, Sonja (1996) *Garlands from Ashes*. Grace-Watson Press, Wanganui

Hermans, Judith Lewis (1992) *Trauma and Recovery*. Pandora, London

Houston, Jean (1992) Godseed, *The Journey of Christ.* Theosophical Publishing Society, Wheaton

Jamieson, Alan (2000) *A Churchless Faith.* Philip Garside, Wellington

Johnson, Elizabeth A (1996) *She Who Is.* Crossroad, New York

Jones, Alexander (ed) (1966) *Jerusalem Bible D*arton, Longman Todd, London

Jung, Carl G (1938) *Psychology and Religion.* Oxford University Press, UK

Jung, Carl G (1963) *Memories, Dreams, Reflections.* Aniela Jaffé (ed) Fontana Paperbacks, London

Kelly, G (1958) *Catholic Marriage Manual.* Robert Hale, London

Leech, Kenneth (1972) *Soul Friend, A Study of Spirituality.* Sheldon Press, London

McDowell, Josh (1977) *More than a Carpenter.* Tyndale House, US

Nicholl, Donald (1981) *Holiness.* Seabury Press, NY

Nolan, Albert (1977) *Jesus Before Christianity, The Gospel of Liberation.* Darton, Longman Todd, London

Ormerod, Neil (1992) 'Grace and Disgrace: A Theology of Self-Esteem.' In *Society and History.* E J Dwyer (ed) Newtown, NSW, Australia

Ormerod, Neil and Thea (1995) *When Ministers Sin – Sexual Abuse in the Churches.* Millennium Books, NSW, Australia

Ross, Isabel (1949) *Margaret Fell, Mother of Quakerism.* William Sessions Ltd, UK

Rutter, Peter (1989) *Sex in the Forbidden Zone.* Jeremy P Tarcher, Los Angeles

Schaeffer, Ulrich (1979) *Into Your Light.* Intervarsity Press, Leicester, UK

Schoener, Gary, Milgrom, Jeanette et al. (1989) *Psychotherapists' Sexual Involvement with Clients: Intervention and Prevention.* Walk-in Counseling Center, Minneapolis

Skolomowski, Heinrich 'The Journey of the Evolutionary God,' based on book: *A Sacred Place to Dwell.* Geering Lectures, St Andrew's Trust (2000), Wellington

The Kairos Theologians (1985) *'The Kairos Document, Challenge to the Church.'* The Catholic Institute for International Relations and The British Council of Churches, London

Endnotes

1   Frame, Janet (1985) 'The Place.' In *The Penguin Book of New Zealand Verse*. Ian Wedde and Harvey McQuenn (eds) Penguin, Auckland. p297

2   *The God Book: Talking about God today*. (2008)
    A Thinkers guide to Sin: Thinking about wrong-doing today. (2010)
    Journeying into Prayer. (2012)
    But is it Fair?: Faith Communities and Social Justice. (2014)
    Living in the Planet Earth: Faith Communities and Ecology. (2016)
    All edited by Neil Darragh. Accent Publications, Auckland.

3   Fowler, J W (1995) *Stages of Faith: the Psychology of Human Development and the Quest for Meaning*. Harper. San Francisco. p173. (First published in 1981.)

4   de Mello, Anthony (1985) One Minute Wisdom. Anand Press p23

5   Bausch, W J (1984) *Storytelling, Imagination and Faith*. Twenty-third Publications. pp114-115

6   For example: Rutter, Peter (1990) *Sex in the Forbidden Zone*. Mandala

7   Beesing, Maria, et al. (1984) *The Enneagram, a Journey of Self Discovery*. Dimension Books. p211

8   The Book of Daniel, ch 13. *Jerusalem Bible*. 1966

9   Lytollis, Sue (1983) *Self Defence for Women*. New Women's Press. p20

10 Matthew 27:25. *Jerusalem Bible*. 1966

11 *The Women's Bible Commentary*. Newsome, CA and Ringe SH. SPCK 1992. p867

12 Rutter, Peter (1990) *Sex in the Forbidden Zone*. Mandala. p142

13 Daniel 13:6

14 'A Pastoral Report to the Churches on Sexual Violence Against Women and Children of the Church Community.' Casa House, Melbourne. 1990. pp30-31

15 The blind man holding the leg said 'the elephant is like a tree.' 'No, no' said another blind man holding the trunk, 'the elephant is like a serpent.' 'No,' said another holding the tail, 'the elephant is like a rope.' 'No,' said another blind man holding the ear, 'the elephant is like a sail.' And they fought about who was wrong and who was right.

16 'Renew' was a nationwide programme of faith-sharing groups in the Catholic Church in the late 1980s

17 Tertullian was an early church father/theologian (c160 – c225)

18 St Augustine of Hippo, Doctor of the church (354 – 430)

19 Eliot, T S (1944) 'Little Gidding.' In Four Quartets. Faber and Faber, London

20 An independent Catholic monthly magazine

21 From Hebrew, meaning the down-trodden ones

22 Jamieson, Alan (2000) *A Churchless Faith*. Philip Garside, Wellington

23 The seven sacraments of the Catholic tradition

24 Reproduced from: Walsh, J (1982) *Evangelization and Justice, New Insights for Christian Ministry*. Orbis Books. New York

Glossary

Note: Māori, along with English, is an official language in Aotearoa New Zealand. Many Māori words are now used in everyday speech.

Aotearoa — Land of the Long White Cloud

aroha — love

arohanui — much love

karanga — a chant of greeting and welcome performed by women

koru — coiled stage of a fern frond

mana — dignity, personal worth

rangatira — leader, chief

toitoi — tall grass similar to pampas

tūī — native bird with bell-like call

tūrangawaewae — home-ground, standing place

whānau — extended family

About the Author

Trish McBride was born in Lancaster, England and came to Aotearoa New Zealand in 1952. For most of her life she was deeply involved in the Catholic Church. She has subsequently spent times with ExAlt, a women's spirituality group, a Progressive Presbyterian parish, and the Religious Society of Friends, and now identifies as post-denominational.

Now retired, Trish has been a spiritual director, chaplain in various contexts, counsellor and supervisor. She is mother to 7 and delighted grandmother to 23, some acquired, and is now (2024) happily settled in a retirement village.

A high point in her writing career was as a prize-winner in a 1994 international competition for religious journalism awarded by *The Tablet*, London. Others have been contributing chapters to five Aotearoa Catholic-based theology books, (*The God Book*, *A Thinkers Guide to Sin*, *Journeying into Prayer*, *But is it Fair?* and *Living in the Planet Earth*), publication of two academic papers in USA, and completing her own unintended trilogy: *Faith Evolving*, *Exploring the Presence* and *A Love Quilt*.

Many of the articles and poems in her books have previously appeared in a variety of publications. Formal studies included MA (Hons) in Classics, Diploma in Pastoral Ministry and Recognition as an Associate in Christian Ministry (interdenominational).

Involvements include family, social justice, nurturing friendships, quilting, reading, swimming, walking and occasional painting.

About the book

How is religious faith affected by our life's experiences? Trish McBride started with a traditional Christian faith. Over time this has evolved into a belief in a God who is free of denominational church boundaries. One poem and prose step at a time, Trish weaves the scattered patches of her life into a compelling narrative that will touch your heart, and invite you to ponder your own faith journey.

"This book is divided into three sections, each prefaced with a reflection on how she perceives, retrospectively, her faith journey:

- Clothes-line Theology: 1974 – 1986

- After That: 1987 – 1994

- Tūrangawaewae: 1995 – 2005

The young adult Trish, who strived to fulfil the expectations of a traditional [Christian] marriage and parish, has passed through the crucible of pain and loss by 2005 to become a mature and joyful Trish. The God, who at the beginning is a demanding figure evoking total blind surrender, is by the end the One who seeks justice in solidarity with marginalised women and men, and who manifests not only in creation, but also as the Quiet within."

Anne Hadfield PhD, author and spiritual director

"My God is a God who engages with me as I have wrestled with the hard questions of the realities of my own life and those of other women, a God who has been willing to be present to me in ways that have evolved with my maturing, a God who is firmly on the side of marginal people.

Trish from the Preface

Praise for Faith Evolving

"*Faith Evolving: A Patchwork Journey* is both spiritual biography and contextual theology. It is a work so much more contextual and potentially valuable for us in Aotearoa New Zealand than even those other great writings by Teresa of Avila or Gregory of Nyssa.

Using poems and articles, Trish McBride charts her journey over a thirty-year period from her identity and participation in the Catholic Church to her spiritual search elsewhere. The 'patches' of writing from across this time are threaded together with a brief text that connects them to the overall story. They reveal the struggle, courage, commitment and beauty of a woman's intense relationship with God, family, church and community, and the changing character and understanding of those relationships.

Trish engages with philosophical and theological thought, with psychology and developmental theory as she reflects on the meaning of her experiences. Personal and professional encounters with alcoholism, pregnancies, widowhood, HIV / AIDS, sexual abuse by clergy, domestic violence, the mental health arena, and leaving her church have all provoked reflection. This book is a contribution to theological conversation in the context of Aotearoa New Zealand.

Although *Faith Evolving: A Patchwork Journey* is a personal account, it mirrors the experiences and stories of other women in and beyond the Christian churches of Australasia. Though these churches provide person-al and community support through liturgical and spiritual nourishment, they are also responsible at times for heartbreakingly abusive attitudes and behaviour towards women and children. Trish reveals some of this underside and some of the healing that is probably never enough. However, the author's voice is not bitter or unforgiving – it is much more compassionate and prophetic."

Dr Ann Gilroy, School of Theology, The University of Auckland

"A work of scholarship … profound, with wonderful everydayness and simplicity that shine through."

Helen Simmons, Women's Studies Journal, spring 2006

"Fine, rich writing filled with metaphor and symbol."

Mel Bogard, Friends' Newsletter, April 2006

"A book to enjoy only if one is prepared to savour, mull over and meditate on it. I warmly recommend it."

Sr Mary Scanlon, LCM, Wellington

"Trish McBride has a sharpened awareness of someone who is sensitively in touch with the God who embraces every moment of her life. Her engaging book tells the power of story and the gift of the reflected life."

Joan McFetridge, Tui Motu, Nov. 2005

"Common threads – how amazing to read someone else's story and find in it your own! Trish has journeyed from charismatic community, parish ministry and contemplative explorations through a crisis which propelled her into more radical questioning of the status quo. She is at home now, accompanied by friends, with a faith beyond church and institution.

Trish points out, through use of James Fowler's 'stages of faith' that her story is also that of all who have gone on a spiritual quest – it is a path well-travelled, though sadly rarely understood by those within the church. Many have found that to keep travelling they have to leave the church that nurtured them and find other companions on the Way. Among those companions are books such as Faith Evolving: A Patchwork Journey – in them we see our own stories reflected, and known that we are not alone."

Rosemary Neave, futurechurch

Books by Trish McBride

Trish's three books – *Faith Evolving, Exploring the Presence* and *A Love Quilt* – are being republished in 2024. Read together, they document Trish's 75-year life and faith journey from childhood to her 80s – a unique longitudinal record of women's spirituality and thinking. They are both spiritual biography and contextual theology.

Along the way, Trish moves from a traditional Catholic faith to embracing feminist theology and on into a post-denominational, inclusive, integrated Gospel-centred spirituality. She has used a patchwork metaphor across all three books, connecting writings of many colours, shapes and textures. Her purpose in all three has been to encourage others to ponder and record their own faith journeys.

Available in Print and as eBooks (in PDF, ePub and Kindle-Mobi formats)
Order Trish's books at: www.philipgarsidebooks.com

Faith Evolving: *A Patchwork Journey*
3rd edition – Republished – 2024

How is religious faith affected by our life's experiences? Trish McBride started with a traditional Christian faith, which evolved into a belief in a God who is free of denominational boundaries. The various 'patches' of 30 years of life-faith poems, prayers and stories have become a compelling story that will touch your heart and invite reflection.

Exploring the Presence: *More Faith Patches*
Republished – 2024

The passionate, rich and honest story of a woman who left her church after awakening to the Divine Feminine. Trish honours the Presence of the Holy One who permeates All that Is, however we may name Her / Him, in an authentic expression of women's spirituality. A fearless spiritual exploration of other ways of knowing.

A Love Quilt: *Later Faith Patches*
Republished – 2024

A compilation of later-life writings from Trish's 75-year spiritual journey, blending Christian spirituality and unorthodox ideas on matters such as love, inter-faith, race, social justice, and science. Stories, poems, and liturgies to inspire you on your journey, encourage you and provoke thoughtful reflection.

www.ingramcontent.com/pod-product-compliance
Lightning Source LLC
Chambersburg PA
CBHW080957120626
46546CB00010B/2925